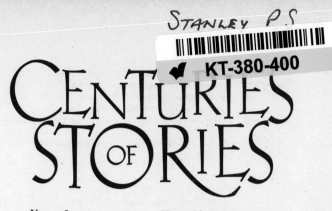

NEW STORIES FOR A NEW MILLENNIUM

Centuries of Stories first published in Great Britain in hardback by Collins in 1999
This edition published in paperback by Collins in 2000
Collins is an imprint of HarperCollins*Publishers* Ltd,
77 - 85 Fulham Palace Road, Hammersmith, London W6 8JB

The HarperCollins website address is www.**fire**and**water**.com

3 5 7 9 8 6 4

In Ancient Time © Michael Morpurgo 1999
Into the Dark © Henrietta Branford 1999
The Wall © Vivian French 1999
The Valley of the Crocuses © Jean Ure 1999
Wistan the Strange © Robert Swindells 1999
A Taste of Freedom © Mary Hoffman 1999
Angel to Angel © Annie Dalton 1999
Odin's Day © Melvin Burgess 1999
Brother Aelred's Feet © Gillian Cross 1999
The Hammer and the Cross © Alan Durant 1999
A Falcon for a Queen © Theresa Breslin 1999
The Mask © Bernard Ashley 1999
The Death of a Prince © Jenny Nimmo 1999
'Why Would I Lie?' © Geraldine McCaughrean 1999
The Mystery of the Invisible Friends © Pete Johnson 1999
The Daughter © Jacqueline Wilson 1999
London Rises from the Ashes © Jeremy Strong 1999
Toinette © Adèle Geras 1999
North © Oneta Malorie Blackman 1999
Swimming in Time © Margaret Mahy 1999

Collection copyright © Wendy Cooling 1999
Illustrations © David Wyatt, Mark Robertson, Tim Stevens, Sarah Young

ISBN 000 675415 5

Printed and bound in Great Britain by
Clays Ltd, St Ives plc

Conditions of Sale

CENTURIES STORIES OF

NEW STORIES FOR A NEW MILLENNIUM

Edited by Wendy Cooling

Collins

📖 *An imprint of HarperCollinsPublishers*

Contents

✶

For Henrietta Branford
1946-1999

INTRODUCTION

✦

This collection of stories celebrates two thousand years of storytelling and the strength and magic of contemporary writing for young people. The stories represent the imaginations of twenty brilliant writers, who rose to the challenge offered – to write a story set in one of the last twenty centuries. Most of the authors responded immediately and positively to my invitation; two claimed not to write historical stories but telephoned a day or two later to say they had changed their minds. Their stories are wide-ranging in subject, style, time and place; they give a sense of history as well as a taste of the power of storytelling.

As the first stories began to arrive, I knew that this was to be a very special collection. Reading through them, I was spellbound; transported back in time and round the world. I decided to set aside my initial thoughts of guiding writers towards particular ideas; so the planned story set in a Norman castle became an African tale; a funny story about stories took me instead to the Great Wall of China and this unique collection began to take a shape of its own.

My thanks go to all the writers for the stories and for the pleasure and privilege of working with them. Special thanks to those who had only a few centuries to choose from, and to the one who offered to set her story in the century that no-one else wanted.

My wish is that these stories now give you the pleasure they have given me and that they encourage you to read other work by the contributors. They have all written books that are simply too good to miss, books that offer hours of pleasure and amazement. These stories are for you – readers with much to discover – so please read and enjoy.

Wendy Cooling

1st
CENTURY

———★———

MICHAEL MORPURGO

IN ANCIENT TIME

Illustrated by David Wyatt

Michael Morpurgo

In Ancient Time

When I was young we heard it often, all of us in the village did, but whenever the old man began his story again, we listened rapt all the same. He was blind in his last years, but every time he told the story his eyes blazed as if he was seeing it happen in front of him as he spoke. He finished always with the same words. 'See! He is here! He is here with us now.' And he would point over our heads into the smoky darkness beyond the fire. Time and again I would find myself turning round to look, and I wasn't the only one.

Like the wind through the trees before the rain, we always knew when the story was coming. He would wait for a silence around the fire, lean forward warming his hands, and begin.

In ancient time before any of you were even born, I was a young man. No cursed Roman soldier had yet set foot in this land of ours. We were not then a beaten people. We were wild perhaps, quarrelsome certainly, but we were our own people.

My mother died in giving birth to me, and my beloved father fed me, taught me and protected me. Wherever I went I walked in his steps. He was a god to me. Then one day, whilst I was still only a small boy, he went off hunting into the forest with his brother my uncle, and did not return. He had been attacked by a bear and taken off. Not a bone was ever found of him. That was what they told me.

My uncle, who had no children of his own, took me in, and at once treated me as his slave. I gathered his firewood for him. I set his traps. I skinned his deer. I ground his corn. He was a giant of a man with arms like tree trunks, and the neck of a bull, and he had a raging temper too. It was not until I was nearly a man myself that I at last found the courage to stand up to him, to protest at how I had been used all these years.

'You whining wretch,' he cried. 'Have I not fed you, clothed you, kept you warm through the winters?' And in his fury he took a great staff and beat me to the ground. Blow upon blow he rained down on me. I curled up like a hedgehog to protect myself. I would have stayed there cowering in the dirt. But as he struck me he began to shout at me, a vicious curse with each blow, with each kick. And then after the curses came these terrible words: 'I killed your miserable father, kicked him to death in the woods till there was no breath left in him. Like you, he too turned on me, and enraged me. Like this I killed him, and this, and this, and then left him to the bears and the wolves. So I will leave you. Your blood shall join his blood.'

Vengeance gave me all the strength I needed. With a scream of anger, I rose up and tore the staff from his grasp. I struck him about the body, about the head, until he fell on his knees and begged me to stop. But I did not stop until he was stretched out lifeless at my feet. I ran then, stumbling into the forest, knowing full well that after what I had done I would never see my childhood friends again, nor ever return to my village; that I would wander an outcast for ever, alone all my life, a killer man, a cursed man.

I went west towards the setting sun, and after many weeks, found myself high on a windswept moor, in amongst the sacred mounds where great chieftains lie buried, the sea about me on both sides. It was a darkening winter's evening. The howling cold bit into my bones and froze my spirits. For some days I had had little or nothing to eat, and no shelter either. I was a lost man, filled with remorse at my terrible crime, with nowhere to lay my head, no-one to comfort me. I saw no hope, no end to my suffering. I wandered wailing in my misery through the high bracken that whipped me about the face and the grasping gorse that ripped at my clothes and at my flesh beneath, until at last I came to the edge of a towering cliff with the sea surging far below me. Here, I thought, here I shall end my life for it is not worth the living. I would be resolute. I would be brave. I stepped forward, but found that I could not jump, that my legs would simply not obey me.

I felt a sudden hand on my shoulder.

'Friend,' said a voice. I turned.

He was a man still young, but older than I was, taller

too and with a darker skin. He had eyes that looked into my very soul. 'Come,' he said, and putting his arm around my shoulders, he led me away from the cliff edge. I found I had neither the will nor the power to resist him.

'You need food. You need warmth. You shall stay with my uncle and me,' he said. 'We live close by. It's not much of a place to live, but it is out of the rain, out of the mists. We have a warming fire and there'll be food enough and plenty for another one. Come.'

So they took me in. He called himself Jesus, Jesus of Nazareth, and his old uncle I came to know as Joseph of Arimathea. I had heard of neither place. They were travellers, they told me, who had come from an eastern land across the sea. They had come as far west as they could and were working in a tin mine nearby. It would be hard work, they said, but they could always do with help, with another strong back, another pair of hands. So, for a winter, a spring and a summer, the three of us lived together, and side by side hammered and hewed in the tin mine. My spirits were restored and my strength too. I lacked for nothing: food, water, shelter, and most welcome of all, human companionship.

There was often silence between us, but it was the

silence of friends at ease with one another. Jesus and Joseph seemed often deep in meditation and prayer, and more and more I found myself drawn into their ways. When they did talk they spoke of such wonders, such places and people as I could never have imagined. From them I first heard of the Romans, who already ruled their country and much of the rest of the world too it seemed. It was a rare and wonderful thing, they said, to come to a place where the Romans did not rule. They had been as far east as they had west on a great voyage of discovery. They talked of mountains as high as the sky itself, of great temples in the clouds of the east, of wise men and visionaries they had encountered in their travels. But most often they told me of their God, a god so powerful that he would one day prove stronger than even the mighty Romans themselves, and yet at the same time a merciful god who loved us and forgave us when we did wrong.

I listened in wonder to all of this – Jesus was a man I had to listen to, I wanted to listen to – and in time I began to ask questions, for there was much I did not understand. 'Who is this god you speak of? Where is he? Where will I find him?'

'He is in me,' Jesus replied. 'He is in my uncle

Joseph, and he is in you too. He is in all of us, if we want him to be.'

In all this time neither Jesus nor his uncle Joseph ever asked why I had come there or how it was that I had been found in so wretched a state, ready even to kill myself.

We were sitting silent around the fire one autumn evening. I was filled with remorse, as I always was when contemplating my dreadful crime. I looked up and found them both watching me. There was no accusation in their eyes, only a tenderness, an understanding that moved me at last to speak out and tell them my story. When I had done, Jesus reached out and put his hand on mine.

'Go home where you belong,' he said. 'Your uncle lives. I tell you he is not dead.' He spoke with such certainty. 'We will go together, for the time has come when my uncle and I too must go home where we belong. We have wandered long enough in this wilderness. I have God's work to do, and I must wait no longer.'

So early one morning with the autumn mists still shrouding the valleys we set off together. The closer we came to my village the more I worried how I might be received, and the more I began to doubt Jesus' assurances that I would find my uncle was still alive. We parted by the river below the village, in the shadow of the great alder trees where the salmon lie low in the pools. I was fearful, and reluctant to leave my companions. I urged them to accompany me into my village.

'Go on alone, friend,' Jesus whispered as he embraced me. 'All shall be well.'

'If ever you need us, come to Palestine. You will find us easily enough,' said Joseph. And they left me to find my own way.

It was as Jesus had said. My uncle was indeed alive. More than that, he was a changed man, utterly changed. He fell on his knees at once, begging me for forgiveness before the whole village. I could see that he meant it, that all the fury and cruelty had gone out of him. I forgave him readily, knowing only too well what agony of remorse he had been through. There was great feasting and rejoicing that night, for I had long been supposed dead.

But despite all my uncle's kindnesses to me – he treated me with great affection after my return, like a long lost son – I found myself restless, no longer content to stay all my life in my village. I longed to go to Palestine, to be with Jesus and Joseph again. So after only three summers at home I set off on my own voyage of discovery. I travelled over the sea into Gaul, to Rome itself, then by ship again to Egypt and across the desert at last to Palestine.

The closer I came the more I heard of Jesus of Nazareth, how his words touched the hearts of the people, of the poor and the downtrodden, how he had given hope where there was none. Some said he made miracles. Some were calling him 'the Messiah'. Some said he would set them free and drive the Romans from their land forever. He was on his way to Jerusalem, they said.

So I went at once to Jerusalem to meet him. There were very few people about. I asked after him in the market place. They just laughed at me and told me I had better hurry.

'Why?' I asked.

'Why do you think there's hardly anyone here in the market? Always the same when they crucify someone – half the city goes to watch – ruins our trade. It's all his fault, that Jesus of Nazareth. It's him they're crucifying, him and a couple of thieves.'

'Where?' I could scarcely find my voice.

'Golgotha,' they told me and pointed up the hill. 'Outside the city walls. Just follow the crowd.'

So I did. I joined the surge of the crowd as they packed the narrow streets, pushing and jostling my way through until at last I found him. He was staggering under the weight of his cross, Roman guards whipping him on like a donkey as he went. Someone had pressed a cruel crown of thorns on to his head and his face was running with blood.

Our eyes met, and he knew me at once. He smiled through his pain. 'All shall be well, friend,' he said. Swept along by the crowd, I followed. I was there when they nailed him to his cross and raised him high. Those same accursed Romans that now infest every corner of our land stood there and mocked him in his agony. But Jesus shouted no curses at them. He simply said:

'Father, forgive them. Father, forgive them.'

He took all night to die. In the cold grey of dawn as I sat huddled under my cloak, my eyes filled with tears of anger, tears of grief, I felt a hand on my shoulder.

'Come, friend, we have seen enough. Come away.'

It was his uncle Joseph, Joseph of Arimathea. We left Jerusalem that same morning. It was not safe to stay. Every one of Jesus' friends was being sought out and hunted down. In fear of our lives we moved from village to village, travelling only by night, and hiding by day.

One day, hiding out in the dark depths of a mountain cave, he showed me the cup for the first time. 'This cup,' he told me, 'is the very cup Jesus drank from at the last supper he ate with his friends. I shall hide it somewhere where it will be safe, safe for ever.'

Joseph was very old and frail by now, and I knew that he could not keep running for much longer.

'Let's go home, Joseph,' I said. 'Let's go back to my land, my village. There are no Romans there. We'll be safe. The cup will be safe.'

He was too exhausted to argue. The journey home was long and arduous, so it was nearly winter before we came home at last. And for one short autumn we lived here together, Joseph and I, in my uncle's house. Never a day went by that we did not speak of Jesus. We drank from his cup every evening at supper – it was one way we could feel close to him. To both of us the world seemed such an empty place without him.

Sometimes Joseph liked to walk up the Tor at Glastonbury to watch the sunset. He found the climb hard, and often had to lean heavily on his staff. We were up there at the top one evening as the world went dark around us.

'Bury me here on this hill, friend,' he said, 'with Jesus' cup beside me. He is here with us now. Can you feel him?' And I could. I could.

When the time came, I did as he had asked me. I laid him in the soft earth of Glastonbury Tor, set the cup from the last supper in his hands and filled his grave. As I walked away, I drove his staff into the ground and left it there.

I did not go back until the snows came. At the very place I had left his staff there now grew a hawthorn tree, covered in white blossom. It is still there to this day. Blind as I am, I can see it now, as I can see Jesus. See! He is here! He is with us now.

The old man died many long years ago, and I myself am now as old as he was. The Romans are still here, but one day they will be gone and we shall be our own people again. The hawthorn tree still blossoms on Glastonbury Tor in the depths of every winter, and rest assured, it always will. Now it is I who sit by the fire and tell the old man's story to the young ones. Each time I tell it, I feel as if I am passing on something precious, more precious even than the cup that still lies buried somewhere on Glastonbury Tor.

2nd
CENTURY

———— ✶ ————

HENRIETTA BRANFORD

INTO THE DARK

Illustrated by Mark Robertson

HENRIETTA BRANFORD

INTO THE DARK

I was born out of doors, I think, under the tall green bracken or out on the bee-singing heather. My mother loved such places. She died when I was very small but I remember her. She loved me and held me close. She did not want to leave me. She was one of the lake people, and our house was built on stilts, over the water. All night the lake lap-lapped under our floor.

When my mother died I was taken in by a woman called Marne who moved me away from the lake to live beyond the forest. I got no love from her – cold food and a cold heart, that was her way. Blows and curses. Goban, her man, was worse. Many's the time I thought he'd kill me. I used to think that if I did what they wanted, they would take to me, but they never did. They wanted my labour, not me.

That's why they sent me to carry the warning. It was a simple message: the Romans are coming, clanking up the hillsides, tall as giants. This is our land, but their general Hadrian has ordered the building of a great wall across it, to keep us away. It never will. They may be powerful and strong, with their gods and their roads and their long, long marches, but this is our land and we'll keep it.

I was to run to the lake. They said I must run all night and not stop until I'd warned the lake people. I said: 'It will be night time, and dark.' They laughed.

Marne and Goban were grabbing what they could carry and running north almost before I left them. 'How will I find you when I'm done?' I asked. They didn't answer.

'Head for the river and sundown,' the head man told me. 'Cross where the rocks make stepping stones. Follow the stream through the wood. You'll find the village on an island in a lake.'

He did not give me a knife or a spear. I had no wool cloak and no shoes either. I do not like the dark. It presses on me and makes me afraid. The spirits of the dead love darkness. So do the priests, whom everybody fears. Also the wolf and the boar and the bear.

As I left the village, mad Mab tottered out of her hut and laid her bony hand on my head. She wiped a sign on to my forehead with her thumb. Writing is forbidden to us. Only the priests may write. I felt afraid, but I trusted her, because on those nights when Marne threw me out, or when I had to run from Goban's fist, I ran to Mab and she would let me in. Mostly she had no food and no fire, but she let me stay with her. I said goodbye to her and she kissed me. Then I ran towards the river.

Smell of the bog myrtle as I push through the bushes. Smell of mint, and the water close by. I reach the river just as dusk wraps the land in mystery. The rocks are slippery and the water's deep. Water will suck you under if it can. Wait until the sun is gone. Now the sky is red like blood. Fish rise to catch the last of the dancing flies. Deer step out of the wood to drink at the river. Maybe an old grey wolf follows behind. Watch where the evening star will rise.

That star will show me the way. They told me not to

stop but how can you run if you don't know the way? *Moonlight, starlight, bad'uns won't come out tonight.* I think my mother taught me that. Here is my star now. Look to the oak tree. Mark where the sun goes down. See where the star comes up. Now run.

Deer scatter when I stand. The dark is thicker now. River plants, cold under my foot, give off a good clean scent.

I run under the trees and the dark is all around me. These are yew trees. When the priests cut mistletoe from the yew they sacrifice to Lugh. I don't want their sacred knives digging in my entrails.

Water beside me. Look for the star in every clearing. Run until my lungs hurt and my heart hammers. Stop, breathing hard and loud. Quiet, quiet. I'll sit and rest a moment. I hear the song of water over stones. My eyes close. Only for a moment. Then I'll run again.

Wake to the sound of footfalls in the dark. Two priests come down to the water. No one can hide from them, they can see in the dark. What will they do to me? I make myself small and quiet and pray to Macha our mother to protect me. They lean over the water, killing something small they take from a sack. When they have finished they go back the way they came. They don't want me. I stand up, stretch, and run.

Wolves call to one another in the moonlight, long, shivering wails. I run under holly trees, the prickles sting my bare feet. After the prickle is out, the sting remains. I will run round them. Where is the water? I have lost the stream. The wolves are coming close, very close. Is it me they're hunting?

A yip in the dark, ahead of me. Another behind me. Climb like a cat up the ivy on a big oak tree. I sit on a broad branch, high above the pathway, with my legs drawn up tight. An old grey wolf trots out of the bracken. He stands under my tree, looking up. Moonlight shines on his long teeth. His mate comes out from under the bracken and stands beside him, staring at me. She is asking me a question but I don't know what it is. Now comes a long cry, a hunting cry, from off behind. Old man wolf and his mate run away into the darkness. It wasn't me they wanted.

I sit in the tree, shaking. From here I can see past the wood and down into the valley. There's a fire down there. Firelight shines on the helmets of the Romans. They clothe themselves in iron, it makes them hard to kill. I must move quietly. If they catch me they'll kill me. If they kill me, the lake people die too. I want to stay safe in my tree. I want to warn my mother's people. I want to hide. I want to run. Cloud covers the moon, the wood grows pitchy black. Down in the valley the fire glows red. Goban would stay in this tree. Goban has no pride, no courage, no love for anyone. But I am not like him. I remember how my mother loved me.

I scrabble down the ivy. The moon sails out to light my way. I run down to the valley, moving quietly, carefully round the camp. A dog barks. Guards pace inside their palisade. They do not see the boy running past in the dark.

Ahead, the lake shines like a silver dish. I stand and stare while my fear and my anger and my sorrow rise in my chest and take my breath away. I think of my mother, take a deep breath and run downhill and out on to the wooden causeway. My feet thud, the wood is wet, I trip and roll over. I have not fallen all my long run, but now I fall like a fool, thumping down on my arse, ringing the wooden causeway like a bell.

A man runs out and hauls me up by the elbow. He brings his spear up under my chin. 'Who are you?' he whispers. 'Tell me, before I kill you.' His spear pricks sharp into my neck.

Before I can answer, a door opens in a house close by

and a woman steps out. She walks over to where I crouch, the spear at my neck. She puts out her hand to trace the sign on my forehead. 'Leave him,' she says. 'He's a friend.'

'I'm from beyond the wood,' I say. I do not tell them that I came from here, once. 'I've run all night.'

'What for?' asks the woman. The man's spear is close to my neck still.

'To tell you the Romans are coming. They're camped close by in the valley. I was sent to give you time to run.'

'Run now, fight later,' says the man. He takes his spear away from my neck. 'What kind of people send a boy, alone and unarmed, without shoes on his feet, to warn their neighbours of danger?' he asks. The woman shakes her head and sighs. I feel ashamed.

After that the man put his hand on my shoulder and brought me indoors. His name was Vran. He gave me food and I sat in the warm, eating and drinking, while Vran spoke to the woman. When they went out to wake the village, I slept. I dreamed I had a proper home, where I could sit by the fire and eat when I was hungry. A stupid dream, I thought when I woke up.

Vran came in soon after. 'We're going now,' he said.

'So am I,' I answered.

He looked at me. 'I see a boy with nowhere good to go,' he said. 'I know that look.'

That was a long while back. I am at home in Vran's house now – one of the Lake people again. But I still remember running through the dark, and meeting Vran on the causeway.

3rd
CENTURY

───★───

VIVIAN FRENCH

THE WALL

Illustrated by David Wyatt

VIVIAN FRENCH

THE WALL

I was always aware of the wall. Even when I was a tiny girl child strapped to my grandmother's back I would stare and stare at it as we rode past. It was so high! Twelve men standing on each other's shoulders couldn't reach the top... a monstrous barricade of mud and stone and rock and pebbles. When I was old enough to listen, my brothers told me tales of snakes and dragons and terrible flesh-eating monsters that lived on the other side, and I was glad of its size and strength. It stormed

out from the mists where the sun rose in the morning
and stretched across my whole world, and was only lost
to view in the shadows where the sun set at night.
Sometimes when we moved to the higher ground I could
see it marching over the mountains. It must, I thought,
go on for ever.

At first I thought the wall was like the earth, or the
trees, or the moon… something that had always been
there. It was only as I grew older that I began to
understand that it had been built by men. But who?
And why? And gradually I realised something else. The
wall made my father angry. To me that seemed the
strangest thing of all. Didn't the wall give shade to the
horses when the midsummer sun was blazing down?
Didn't it mark, clearly and emphatically, the end of the
lands where we were safe? When I slipped away from the
tents to go walking on my own I was never lost. The
wall was always there to show me the way back to
wherever we had set up our camp that night. In places it
twisted away from being the long straight line that
snaked across the grassy plains. When the winter winds
were howling and raging we could move our tents close
against it and avoid the worst of the cutting icy teeth of
the North. I was glad of the shelter of the wall and so

was Grandmother Pearl, but my brothers laughed.

'When the old one dies we'll never come near the wall again,' they boasted. 'And you, Little Rabbit – you must learn to bear the wind in winter and the sun in summer, or you'll never be a true daughter of the horse herders.'

I wasn't sure I wanted to be a true daughter if it meant I had to freeze in the winter and scorch in the summer, but I didn't say so. My brothers were too big.

I went on wondering about my father's anger. I never asked him. He was the kind of man who told you what to do, not the sort of man to discuss feelings. The only time he ever talked gently was when he was calming a frightened horse. Sometimes I thought my grandmother and I would have had an easier life if we'd had four hooves and a mane and tail. But maybe not. When my father cracked his long leather-thonged whip, every horse in the herd – even the raw-boned youngsters – did exactly as he told them. Me too. He was far quicker to beat me than he was to beat the silly little foals with their fluffy coats and wobbly legs. Foals grew up to be brood mares and stallions that he could sell for pieces of gold or silver. Me? I was Little Rabbit, and would never amount to anything. Even though I was wiry and strong

I was only a girl. It was my duty to walk behind my father, tend the fire, sweep the tents, bake the bread, and look after Grandmother Pearl.

Why didn't I ask Grandmother Pearl the questions that filled my head? All the questions about the wall? I did, sometimes… but she never answered. She was old – very old. I think perhaps she was my mother's grandmother, or maybe even older, and her mind floated free like the clouds in the sky. When my mother died she looked after me, but even then she sometimes thought I was one of her own daughters… all of whom had died long ago. I was sorry that she never answered my questions, but I listened open-mouthed when she told me her stories – wonderful stories of strange places, and a strange people who lived a different life from us.

'They do not move from place to place,' Grandmother Pearl told me. 'They have houses. The houses are made of wood, and of stone. The people who are rich live with many beautiful things. Their clothes are made of the softest silk. The silk shimmers and shines. It is embroidered with butterflies and flowers and wonderful birds. There are little whispering rivers. Gardens with snow-white and rose-pink petalled trees. The old – ' and here Grandmother Pearl would sometimes give a little sideways glance at my father — 'are treated with veneration. They sit and talk, or play music. Some look at the words of poetry painted on to sheets of thin parchment.'

My father, if he was paying any attention at all, would snort loudly at this story. 'Foolishness!' he would shout. 'Nonsense! How can words be painted? Idiocy!'

Grandmother Pearl took little notice of my father's furious interruptions. 'When death comes,' she went on, 'they are dressed in a coat made of pieces of precious jade. They are laid to rest in a funeral house for the dead. Horses and servants are placed beside them. Then the houses are closed up, but they are always cared for. They are cared for by the dead one's children, and their children's friends. They respect the houses of their ancestors... where they belong...' And then she would sigh and mutter a few words that I couldn't understand, and say nothing more for a long time.

The first time Grandmother Pearl told me about the funeral houses I stared at her. What did she mean? How could anyone shut horses inside such a place? But she went on telling the story over the years, and gradually I understood that these were not real horses. They were made of clay, and so were the figures of the servants.

Once, when I was nine or ten summers old, I found a little clay and began to try and model a horse for myself, but my oldest brother found me and beat me soundly for wasting time.

'Grandmother fills your head with nonsense!' he yelled at me. 'What do you need to know of land stealers? When the old one dies and we throw her over the wall we'll teach you what happens to little girls who listen to rubbish – or maybe we'll throw you over too! You can keep her old bones company!'

'WHAT?' I tried to wriggle away, but he held me too tightly. 'What do you mean, throw Grandmother over the wall? There are snakes there! And monsters! You told me!'

It was the first time I had ever surprised my oldest brother. He actually stopped beating me, and stared.

'Little Rabbit!' he said at last. 'You mean you don't know?'

'Know what?' I asked, rubbing my shoulders.

'You don't know that Grandmother Pearl was born one of them? A Han? One of the Han Emperor's people? It was the Hans who stole our land! The evil ones who built the wall so we can't ride our horses over OUR Southern hills and plains!' My brother shook his head at me. 'Didn't you ever wonder why we keep so close to this monster, this stone snake, this devil's pile of rock and stone?'

'No,' I said. I couldn't tell him that I thought the wall was for warmth, and shelter... and even safety.

'All women have weak brains,' my brother growled. 'The old woman wants to go back to the land of her birth. Your mother promised her she would be buried there.' He glared at me as if it was all my fault. 'And our father will keep that promise... even though it'll mean death for him if he's seen on the wall. And so we wait. I believe she stays alive to spite us! But when she does die – then it's over the wall with her, and away we'll go! We'll take the horses where the grass grows deep and strong, and NEVER ride here again.' He clenched his fist. 'Not, that is, until one day all of us beyond the wall come together... and break it down and take back what is ours!' And his eyes glittered as if he was seeing a vision of the future. It made me shiver, so he beat me some more to make me warm.

Perhaps my brother was right. Perhaps I was weak in my brain. After he had left me I sat still, and thoughts whirled round in my head. So – Grandmother Pearl came from the other side of the wall. There were people there – not snakes, or dragons, or monsters. And her stories... surely this meant they were all true? I went on sitting until the moon came up, and the wall shone above me as if it was built of blocks of silver.

It was then that I decided. I was going to climb the wall. I was going to climb the wall, and take Grandmother Pearl with me. I would find someone to care for her; someone who would treat her as she wished to be treated. And I would take her before she died, so that she would know that she had come home at last.

I began to watch as we moved from one grazing place to another, watching the wall almost as if it was a living thing. I looked for rough places, weaknesses, places where the reeds that bound the mortar together had dried and fallen away, places where stones had slipped and fallen – anywhere that I might find a hand and foothold.

Another winter came and went, and then another. I grew taller, but Grandmother Pearl began to fail. More and more often she spoke in words that none of us could understand, and my brothers and my father became more and more impatient with her. Now, instead of Grandmother carrying me on her back as she had done when I was a baby, I carried her. She was so little and light that I worried about the wind picking her up and tossing her away, and I wrapped her tightly in my own felt cloak. When we stopped to make camp I would sit her on the cloak as if she were a small child, and sometimes she would smile at me and sometimes she would stare away into the nothingness of the sky. My brothers talked loudly now about how it would be when they could take the herds of horses away from the wall and into the hills. My father did not stop them.

It was a clear spring evening when I saw the place. We had pitched the tents, and my father was checking the new foals. Soon it would be time to take the pick of them to the crossing of the river where he met other tribesmen, and the selling and bartering went on. Grandmother Pearl was half-sleeping, half-waking by the fire and I was walking beside the wall, picking sorrel to flavour our evening food. And there it was. A deep crack, splitting the outer face from top to bottom. Bushes and shrubs had taken seed in the crevices, and almost covered the gaps and missing stones, but the cleft was wide. I walked a little nearer, and it was good. It would be hard, but I could do it.

Night had never taken longer to come. My father and

brothers worked with the horses until late, and then came to the fires to eat and, finally, sleep. Grandmother Pearl sat unmoving, and once or twice I thought I could see the glow of the flames shining right through her thin frail body.

The moon was covered in a coat of clouds, but there were stars in the deep blue of the sky. The fire burnt down to a steady glow, and I could hear the sound of heavy breathing as my father and brothers slept. Grandmother sat on by the embers. Usually I would have helped her into her sleeping place long before, but she made no sign that she knew that I was late. She did not turn as I wrapped the cloak round her and lifted her.

The climb was hard. Very hard. Although Grandmother was so little I still had to hold her safe on my back with one hand, and once I thought I had lost both of us as a branch tore away beneath my feet. I caught at a root – and I was lucky that it held. I stopped for a moment to gasp for breath, and felt Grandmother's small thin arms creep round my neck and hold on tightly. She began to make a strange, sweet sound – and I realised she was singing. There were no words, only a tiny thread of sound, like the song of a dawn bird.

I took a deep breath, and went on climbing. Sweat

dripped from my forehead and ran, stinging, into my eyes. I couldn't wipe it away. The moon came out from behind the clouds, and that helped me see. Up and up and up I climbed – and then, with a final heave and a gasping for breath, I was there. On the top of the wall. And Grandmother Pearl let go of me, and sang as she looked at the place where she had been born. And I realised, with a sickening lurching of my stomach, that there was no way we could ever get down the other side.

I didn't see the soldier coming. The first I knew was a heavy hand on my shoulder, and a patter of strange words. His grip was painful, and determined. I remembered my oldest brother's words. 'If he's seen on the wall, it means death.' And a cold terror froze me.

I'll never know what Grandmother Pearl said. She put her minute claw of a hand on the soldier's arm and looked at him with her faraway cloudy eyes, and she spoke the words I had heard her use so often when she told me of the funeral houses. And the soldier let me go. He let me go, and he put his hands together and made me a deep bow. Then he picked up Grandmother Pearl as if she was the most precious jewel in the whole wide world, and carried her away. And Grandmother Pearl sang as she went, and I knew she was singing me goodbye, and when her voice faded and stopped I knew it was her goodbye to the world as well. Grandmother Pearl had gone home to her ancestors.

My father was waiting for me as I slid and slithered back down the wall. I arrived at the bottom in a rush of little stones, and waited for his anger to break over my head. Instead, he said nothing. He put out his hand to help me up, and we walked to the tents side by side.

4th
CENTURY

—★—

JEAN URE
THE VALLEY OF THE CROCUSES

Illustrated by Sarah Young

JEAN URE

THE VALLEY OF THE CROCUSES

Crogdene – the valley of the crocuses. Spring was here, and the land a mass of yellow flowers all the way down to the banks of the river.

Caroc and his new hound puppy were playing in the sunshine. His father had given him the puppy. Thrown it at him.

'If you want it so badly, then have it!'

The puppy was one of a litter of three produced by Brenna, his father's favourite hunting dog. It had been a disappointing litter. Two of the pups had died at birth, the third had been born lame. It had a crippled front paw that twisted inwards. Cered, Caroc's father, had been going to drown it. What use was a crippled dog? But Caroc had begged for its life to be spared. It was such a little thing! All squirming and helpless.

Caroc knew what it was like to be squirming and helpless. He knew what it was like not to be wanted. He and his pup were two of a kind, for Caroc had a withered hand and would never be able to join the hunt with his brothers. Sometimes the other boys jeered at him and once they had lain in wait and jumped on him. Caroc had fought. Oh, he had fought! He was not his father's son for nothing. But the other boys were bigger and stronger, and who would have cared if they had done him serious harm? He was of no more use than Brenna's pup with its twisted paw.

It was his sister Fion who had come to his rescue. She had rushed in, shouting, and driven the boys off with a stick. Perhaps Fion would care if they had injured him. But she was the only one.

Fion had spoken up for Caroc when he begged his father for the puppy.

'May he not have it, Father? It would mean so much to him!'

That was when Cered had contemptuously tossed it to him, across the floor of the hut.

'Just keep it out of my way,' he'd growled.

The pup was four months old now. Caroc called her Brave Heart, which made Fion laugh and shake her head.

'She will have need of a brave heart if she is to survive.'

'She will survive,' said Caroc. 'She has me to look after her!'

'Then of course she will live to grow old and wise,' agreed Fion. Secretly she thought that Caroc, too, would have need of a strong heart. Life would not be easy for either of them.

The pup had Brenna's coat, grey and shaggy, like most of the hounds in the village, but none of Brenna's long-legged grace and ease of movement. But to Caroc she was beautiful. He and his Brave Heart went everywhere together. At night they slept in each other's arms. By day they roved the valley, but always keeping an eye on his father's hut down in the village.

Caroc's mother, Eridwen, had warned him:

'Do not venture too far. The times are troubled. Stay close to home.'

There had been talk, in the huts at night, of Saxon hordes ravaging the countryside. The Romans, who had been in the land for as long as anyone could remember, from way back before time, were no longer as powerful as once they had been. Rumour had it that they were preparing to pull out, to sail back across the sea to the place called Rome where they had come from all those centuries ago.

Caroc knew nothing of Rome and very little more of the Romans. He knew that they had constructed great towns, and roads running straight as arrows leading to far-off places, but they were of no importance to him in his daily life.

He had seen Romans, of course. Everyone had seen them, for they came to the village. Caroc had even seen the legions, marching. A sight to stir the blood! But no Roman had ever spoken to him, nor did he ever expect to travel their roads or see their towns. What were Romans to him?

'They keep us safe,' muttered Fion.

The Romans, with their chariots and their shining helmets... arrogantly striding the land, raising taxes, in control. It was hard to imagine life without them. Warlike tribes might rejoice at the thought of their downfall, but there was fear in the hearts of the villagers.

The young boys boasted of what they would do if the painted hordes should come. One of Caroc's brothers, Corwen, declared he would stand his ground and fight them off with dagger and spear. The way he spoke, he made it sound as if he would tackle the whole horde single-handed.

Fion said that she would sooner die than be taken prisoner. They had all heard what the Painted People did with the women they captured.

'You will not be captured!' said Corwen. 'I shall defend you.'

But Fion shook her head. She was a year older than Corwen, and she knew better. If the hordes came, there would be no defence.

'I will fight!' said Caroc; but Corwen curled his lip and Fion laughed.

'You are too young!'

'He is too crippled,' said Corwen.

'He is too young!' Fion turned on him savagely. She had a temper, did Fion. 'Nine years old! He will do no fighting.'

'Maybe they won't come,' said Caroc.

But plans were made, just in case. The hills all around were densely wooded; the entire village could hide in those hills and not be found. The women urged that they should all go – men and women alike, with the children. A handful of farmers would stand no chance against the Saxon hordes.

But some of the men were for staying put; Caroc's father and brothers amongst them. Death, declared Corwen, however bloody, was better than fleeing like a whipped cur.

'Stupid,' muttered Fion, but what did she know? A mere girl!

Deep pits were dug where workmen could bury their precious tools, in the hope of recovering them at a later date. And Caroc was told repeatedly, 'not to venture too far'.

He was playing with Brave Heart on the bank of the river when he saw Fion come running towards him, waving her arms and shouting.

'Caroc, Caroc! Come quickly!'

Caroc scrabbled his way back up the bank, followed by the pup.

'What is it?'

'Quick! It is time!' She caught him by the hand. 'We must go!'

She made to rush him off, but Caroc snatched his hand away from her and scooped Brave Heart into his arms. He wasn't leaving his dog.

'Hurry, hurry!' Fion grabbed his sleeve, hustling him along.

'Put that animal down!' roared Caroc's mother, when she saw him.

'No!' Caroc hugged the pup protectively. With her twisted paw, she would never be able to keep up.

Eridwen hunched shoulders. 'As you please!'

If the boy wished to lag behind and die, then let him. She had more important things to worry about. Eridwen was with child. And this time, may it please the gods, she would give birth to an infant sound in wind and limb; not another cripple.

Caroc ran, as best he could, with Brave Heart in his arms. They had to cross the river and reach the safety of the hills. It was not easy, running across the rough ground and all the time hugging the pup with his one good hand. But she was his dog and he would not abandon her.

Even as they reached the ford, where the water was shallow enough for them to wade across, they could hear the harsh sounds of the Saxon war cries, the terrified lowing of cattle and the clashing of weapons.

'Caroc!' screamed Fion.

She was halfway across the river when she realised he was not with them. He was struggling along behind, with the dog still in his arms.

'*Caroc*!' She turned, and waded back. 'Put her down! Leave her!'

'No!'

Caroc fought, but Fion was too strong. She tore the pup from his grasp and hurled her to the ground, then seized Caroc by the arm and dragged him into the water. Gasping, he had no choice but to stumble after her. The water came up to his knees – up to his waist – up to his shoulders. But at last he was across. He had just the time for one quick look back. The pup was on the river bank, whimpering in fear and bewilderment. Her master had gone and she was left behind! A sob arose in Caroc's throat. What would become of her?

'Come!' Fion was at his side, urging him on. 'It cannot be helped. She must fend for herself.'

But she was too young, and too little. With her twisted paw she would never be able to swim across the river!

'Caroc, this is no time to be thinking of a mere dog.'

Fion took him by his good hand and jerked him roughly forward. 'If you are to survive, you must think of yourself.'

For days and nights – how many, Caroc was unable to tell – they hid in the forest, drinking from streams, eating what they could find or catch. Some of the dogs had come with them and brought down the odd rabbit or squirrel. They managed to stay alive, but their hearts were heavy.

Great leaping flames rose from the valley. By night a red glow could be seen. Caroc knew that it was the village, burning. He knew that the Painted People would have carried off whatever was of value to them, then torched what was left. Probably butchered all the livestock. Set fire to the fields. Killed his father, killed his brothers. But what of Brave Heart?

The thought tormented him. His father had reckoned Caroc a thing of no worth; his brothers, at best, had ignored him. But Brave Heart! She had loved him. She had depended on him. And he had let her down.

As soon as it was thought safe to go back, they crept down the hillside to pick up the pieces of their shattered lives. Caroc had but one thought: to find his pup. Could she have survived, amidst all the death and destruction?

She was not where he had last seen her, on the river bank by the ford. He had been nursing a secret hope that perhaps she might have stayed there, waiting for him to come back.

'Brave Heart!' He called her name and stood, listening. 'Brave Heart! Are you there?'

And then he heard it, the sound of whimpering. It was coming from further down the river. He turned, and ran.

'Brave Heart!' he cried. 'Where are you?'

He found her at last. She was caught in a bed of reeds, tangled up, unable to move. She must have followed him into the river, then lost her footing and been carried downstream. The reeds had saved her from drowning, but she was trembling with fear and bone thin. Caroc could see her ribs, like pieces of twig.

He had to find a way of rescuing her! It was of no use asking Fion or any of the others to help. They were too busy, picking their way through the devastated remains of their village. But he knew that if the pup were not plucked from the water very soon, she would die.

A short way further on there was a willow tree, its leaves trailing in the river. Caroc rushed to it and clambered up. He edged himself out, along one of the branches. It sank down, dangerously low. Caroc stretched out a hand. Brave Heart cried, piteously. But it was no use. He couldn't reach her.

'Brave Heart!' he sobbed. 'Oh, Brave Heart!'

The years moved on. Sixteen centuries came and went. The world entered a new millennium. Crogdene had become Croydon – no longer the valley of the crocuses. Where once the river had flowed, there was thick black tarmac. Where once the crocuses had bloomed there was pavement, grimy and cracked. Buildings stood where the forest had been. Caroc's village, which had grown again, had long since disappeared. A Saxon settlement had sprung up in its place, but that too had gone, centuries and centuries ago, buried beneath the long march of civilisation. Caroc would not have recognised the place where it had stood. Grey concrete covered it, and cars belched fumes into the stale air.

In Old Town, they were pulling down some buildings. A boy called Tom (who for all anyone knew could have been one of Caroc's descendants) had been watching in great excitement from his bedroom window. One day they had come with a bulldozer and crumbled a whole row of houses. Then they had come with a lorry and removed the rubble. Yesterday they had brought what his dad called 'heavy plant' and dug a simply enormous hole. The most enormous hole that Tom had ever seen. They had put a wooden fence all round to stop people getting in there, but from his window Tom could still see the hole. It was so big and so deep he reckoned you could get about a hundred people in it. Ever since they had started digging, Tom had had but one desire: to get behind that fence and have a closer look...

He knew just how he would do it. He had inspected the fence closely: there was a place where it didn't quite reach the ground. A grown-up could never manage to wriggle through. But a boy could.

There was only one problem: Tom's mum had warned him to keep away from that building site.

'It's dangerous,' she said. 'And it's dirty. I don't want you going there.'

But she didn't actually make him promise.

'Mum,' said Tom, on Sunday morning. 'Can I take Prince out?'

Prince was the family dog, a handsome German Shepherd.

'Yes, if you want,' said Mum. 'Where are you going? To the park?'

Tom made a mumbling sound which could have meant yes or could have meant no. Then he slipped Prince on the lead and went racing over the road before his mum could look out of the front room window and see where he was headed.

The workmen weren't there on a Sunday morning; the building site was deserted. First Tom and then Prince squeezed their way under the fence. Now they were safe! Mum wouldn't be able to see them unless she went upstairs and looked out of Tom's window, and she wasn't very likely to do that. Not when she was busy in the kitchen, cooking Sunday dinner. And Dad was out the back, digging a hole of his own. A silly little mimsy hole for planting things in. Not a patch on Tom's hole.

Tom's hole was... magnificent. A hole amongst holes! Tom stood there, gazing down into it. And as he gazed, he was filled with another desire: a desire to fetch a plank, and place it across one corner of the hole, and walk across it.

'Stay there,' he said to Prince. 'On guard!'

Tom trotted off across the building site. Prince sat down by the side of the hole. He had been told to guard it, and guard it he would, though he couldn't quite see what there was to guard. It was just a hole. There was nothing in there. At least, nothing that anyone could see...

But something that a dog could hear!

Prince cocked his head to one side. His ears pricked up. Slowly he rose to his feet. His whole body had suddenly stiffened, on the alert.

What was that?

Tom turned, with his plank.

'Oy! Prince!' he bellowed.

But too late. Prince had taken a flying leap into the hole...

In later years, when he was an old, old man hunkered round the fire, Caroc was fond of telling his grandchildren the story of the Saxon horde; how they had sacked his village and murdered his father and brothers. How he and his sister Fion had run off to hide in the woods. How his pup had tried to follow and had had to be left behind. The part that they loved best, the part they always waited for, was when he told how he had found her again, caught in the reeds and half-dead. How he had edged out on the branch of a willow and risked drowning, but still hadn't been able to reach her.

'How you thought you had lost her,' they prompted.

How he thought he had lost her; but how, all of a sudden, this great dog, like a wolf, had appeared out of nowhere.

'And you were scared!'

'And I was scared,' agreed Caroc. He had feared the wolf was going to take his pup and carry her off.

'But it didn't!'

'No, it didn't.'

Instead, it had picked her up in its mouth and swum with her to the bank, where Caroc had stood, helpless and trembling. It had deposited her – gently! Oh, so gently! – amongst the crocuses, and then disappeared just as suddenly as it had come.

'Like a dream, yet it was no dream.'

'And the pup grew strong!'

'And the pup grew strong,' said Caroc. 'And she became the very best dog that a man could have.'

The story of Caroc and his dog went down in history. It was a tale that was told long after he had gone.

And here was the odd thing. When Prince pulled himself up out of the hole, out of that hole that was dry as a bone, he was dripping wet. And in his collar was caught a yellow flower. A crocus...

5th
CENTURY

—★—

ROBERT SWINDELLS

WISTAN THE STRANGE

Illustrated by Tim Stevens

ROBERT SWINDELLS

WISTAN THE STRANGE

It is exciting but quite safe to play in the Town of Elves
and Giants, because the elves and giants don't live there
now. The houses they built, using stones they cut by
magic and raised with their unimaginable strength,
stand roofless except for the Elfhall, whose roof is also
the floor of a giant's house. The little girls play there all
the time and Wistan would do the same if it were not
for the taunts of the other boys. 'Hey Girlboy,' they
laugh, 'don't forget your doll.'

Wistan has no doll. He's a boy, but he's happier wandering among the ruins trying to picture the everyday lives of giants than he is playing at hunting or fighting. He'd sooner exercise his imagination than his muscles.

Boy or girl, there's one place the children don't go. Ever. Wistan's mother warned him about it as soon as he could walk, and every village child carries the warning in its head. *Stay away from the Dragon's Lair.*

He knows where it is. What it looks like. Has peered at it from a distance in wintertime, when you can see a long way because the trees are bare. It's a house of stones like the ones in the Town of Elves and Giants, except that this one has its roof and it stands on the bank of the stream. Inside is the dragon, guarding the door to the underwater world the elves and giants moved to when they abandoned the town. Wistan's mother says if you go near you hear the dragon growling, but she's never heard it herself. Nobody has except Thorfin the priest, whose task it is to carry the gifts of beads and knives and mutton which ensure that the elves and giants remain content in their watery world, and will never wish to return to the town they built. Thorfin has to stand on the bank, with nothing but the narrow stream between himself and the lair while he casts the gifts into the water. He can hear the dragon growling the whole time, and it is only the secret spells he mutters which prevent the beast from rushing out and devouring him. Wistan is thankful *he'll* never be a priest.

One long afternoon – it is summertime, scorchingly hot – Wistan is sitting on a block of fallen masonry watching the little girls nursing their dolls, when a frightening idea enters his head. He's been brooding over something Ragnar yelled at him earlier. 'When the gods made you they forgot to put in the bravery.' The idea that comes to him is, *if I were to approach the Dragon's Lair, stand where Thorfin stands and hear the growling, it would show that the gods did not forget the bravery, wouldn't it?*

He tries to drive the idea away. It's stupid even to think about. For one thing, there'd be nobody to see him. What's the use of proving your bravery to nobody? Silly idea. A voice inside his head whispers, you'd prove it to *yourself*.

This makes sense to Wistan, though he wishes it did not. He stands, gazing towards the forest. His mouth is dry, his heart a drum. Go on, urges the voice in his head.

You *know* you must, so do it. He finds himself walking slowly towards the trees. His shadow falls across the girls and one of them, Birgit, looks up. 'Where are you going, Wistan?'

The boy shakes his head. 'Nowhere, Birgit.'

'Can I come?'

'Better not, Birgit.'

'Why?'

'Better not, that's all.' He walks on, a part of him wishing Birgit was at his side.

It's murky here, where birches crowd the slope. The sun can't penetrate. There's a green smell that has the proximity of evil in it. The imminence of harm. Wistan shivers, peering between the trunks. Down there flows the stream whose waters wash the Dragon's Lair. *Stay away from the Dragon's Lair.* He shakes his head to drive away the picture of his mother. Moves on down.

And finds the stream. Black water chatters to mossy stones. Shallow here. Deeper down there where it passes the lair. Wistan swallows hard and turns downstream.

A short walk and he stops, ears straining. Water chatter and something underneath, a grumbling, like thunder in the hills. *Wish it was thunder. Thunder's nothing.*

The wind makes a crack in the leaf canopy so that light falls through. It glints on the water, and down there past the dully gleaming holly it slides along the wall of the Dragon's Lair and sparkles in the droplets falling ceaselessly from the great wheel: the giants' wheel, turning by itself to display the power of its makers' magic. Wistan moves on slowly, longs to flee.

The lair comes clear in view as he creeps from trunk to trunk, never taking his eyes off it. He's very close, but not as close as Thorfin the priest when he casts the gifts. *There's* where Thorfin stands, where that splash of sunlight hits the bank. Perhaps it's always there, the sunlight, placed by elves and giants to mark the spot.

Dare I stand in that light, an easy mark for the dragon? Here the growling is so loud Wistan feels it through his shoes. He's close, so very close, yet nothing moves except the wheel, which never stops. He advances, watching the lair, seeking a door that a beast might come through roaring; sees no door. Teetering on one leg he pokes a foot into the shaft of light. Nothing happens. Wiggles it. Still nothing. Sets it down, transfers his weight to it, all the time watching. There comes no roar. No scaly beast. Perhaps his growls are snores.

Wistan knows no spells yet he is standing in

Thorfin's place, unscathed. He breathes deeply, drawing golden light into himself. Little by little his heartbeat slows. He stands gazing at the wheel while his imagination soars toward revelations of such searing brilliance they cause his limbs to shake, as though with fear.

It is a chill autumn morning. The boys, whose taunts have no effect on Wistan now, have taken their toy spears into the hills to try for a hare. The girls, wrapped in hides and homespun, squat with their dolls on a paved area in the Town of Elves and Giants. The wind which plucks at their garments has winter on its breath.

Wistan draws near. Wistan Girlboy. Wistan the Strange, grown more strange since his solitary walk two moons ago. The girls pause in their play, watch his approach. He is carrying something; some object unfamiliar to them. They are curious but unafraid. If there is no manliness in Wistan, there is no cruelty either.

'Little Mothers, I have a thing to show you.' He holds out a contraption of apples and feathers and wood.

Gerda giggles. Wistan the Strange. 'What's it for?'

The lad smiles. 'Watch.'

He holds it at arm's length. Holds it in the wind. Without his touching it the apple starts to revolve on its stick, faster and faster till the feathers are a blurred disc. With moans and cries the girls scramble to their feet and, wide-eyed, back away.

Wistan grins. 'What is the matter, Little Mothers? Why are you afraid?'

Gerda points. 'That… thing. It has magic. You must take it back. Leave it where you found it.'

'The boy shakes his head. 'It has no magic.'

'It *has*. It moved itself.'

'No.' He walks towards the girl, slowly, holding out the object. 'I did not find this, Gerda, I made it. And the wind moved it. It cannot move itself.'

'You made it?' whispers Birgit. 'How?'

'Simple. Look.' He squats, holding the thing on his palm. 'I barked and sharpened this thin straight stick, thrust it through the apple and stuck these five goose quills into the apple, like rays of the sun.' The girls have crept closer. 'The wind pushes the quills and the apple turns on the stick, that's all. No magic.'

'Make it turn again,' murmurs Gretchen. Wistan stands up and holds out the applewheel. It spins. This time the girls do not back away.

'Will you... make one for me?' breathes Birgit.

Wistan smiles. 'Perhaps, later.'

Gerda frowns. 'How... I mean, who showed you how to make it, Wistan, and what's it *called*?'

'It's an applewheel,' says Wistan, 'and nobody showed me. I learned by watching the great wheel on the Dragon's Lair.' He smiled. 'Water will turn the applewheel as well as wind.'

'You went to the *Dragon's Lair*?' gasps Birgit. 'What happened, Wistan? What did you see?'

'I saw a house. A house of stones, like these houses. And a wheel like the applewheel, but bigger.'

'And the dragon? What about the dragon?'

'He was asleep, I think. Listen.' He lowers his voice. 'Shall I tell you a secret?'

'Oooh, yes!'

'It's a deep, deep secret. You mustn't tell *anybody* – not even your mothers. Do you swear?'

'We swear. What's the secret, Wistan?'

'The secret is, there *is* no dragon.'

'No *dragon*? What d'you mean? Why would everybody tell us to keep away if there was no dragon? Of *course* there's a dragon.'

The boy shakes his head. 'There's no dragon, and

that's only *part* of the secret.'

'What's the other part?'

'The great wheel. It was not made by elves and giants. It was made by men, like your father and mine.'

'What?' cries Gretchen. '*That* wheel, taller than three men? You are well named Wistan the Strange! Mad is what you are.'

'There's more,' says Wistan, mildly.

'We want no more,' scoffs Gerda. 'Your head is full of thistlefur. Where *are* the men who did this magic thing? In your dreams, I think.'

Wistan shrugs. 'I don't know where they are, Gerda. They were here, now they're gone.' With a sweep of his arm he indicates the ruins. 'They built this, though I can't tell how. And these stones. These flat stones we stand on. Men carried them here, laid them down so their shoes would stay dry. So that they need not stand in the mud, as we do.'

'So,' Gretchen's gaze is hostile. 'When Thorfin throws gifts in the water, it is for nobody. For nothing. Have you told him?'

Wistan shakes his head. 'No.'

'And your father — does *he* know?'

'I told you — it's a secret.'

'What if I tell my father, and he tells yours? Your skin will smart, I think.'

'You won't tell, Gretchen. You swore.' He smiles. 'One day, a long time from now, we will be like the men who made this town. We will have stone houses and dry shoes and as many great wheels as we care to build. Oh, I see the mockery in your eyes. I know what you are thinking. Wistan. Wistan the Strange. Wistan the *Mad*, most likely. Well then, here's a little more madness for you: I went to the Dragon's Lair to find my bravery but I found something else. I found a path. *Our* path, and it's not like any path we follow now. It doesn't lead to hunting and fighting and killing. It doesn't lure us deeper and deeper into mud till it disappears, leaving us to wallow and drown. It's like *this*.' He slaps the pavement with his shoe. 'Like this, but better.' He starts to walk away then turns, pointing to the dolls. 'Tell *them*,' he cries. 'Tell your babies.'

NOTE

When the Romans withdrew from Britain they left many watermills in working condition. Archaeologists investigating the sites of such mills sometimes find evidence of offerings in the water nearby. It is thought that the peoples who invaded and occupied the land following the Roman withdrawal came upon these mills with wheels turning and machinery grinding. Incapable of working out their use or their origin in human technology, they decided they were the work of demons, and propitiated them with offerings till, after many years the wheels rotted and disintegrated and the machinery ground to a halt.

6th
CENTURY

— ✶ —

MARY HOFFMAN

A TASTE OF FREEDOM

Illustrated by Mark Robertson

MARY HOFFMAN

A TASTE OF FREEDOM

'Come on Con – you promised!' The girl, half-laughing, half-weeping with frustration, tugged at her foster-brother's sleeve.

The young man, a few years older than her, shook his head in mock-exasperation. 'You know if I do we'll both get into trouble, Mara.'

But he knew that he would give in; he *had* promised, in a weak moment, to help his foster-sister with her crazy scheme, and he was a man of his word. He,

Constantine, son of Cador, had to maintain the family honour. But what if Mara's exploit brought disgrace on the family? Con could imagine his father's wrath.

'What about your hair?' Con asked, playing for time. 'You can't cut it, and you can't pass for a boy with those lovely tresses.'

He twined his hand in Mara's light red-gold braids and tugged. They wrestled and laughed together like real brother and sister, but Con was aware he was playing a dangerous game. He was already half in love with this unruly girl, but he knew that neither of them could choose their future mate. Duke Cador of Cornwall would do that.

That was why Mara was desperate for this adventure. She had overheard rumours in her foster-father's hall that she was to be married soon. She would do what Cador decided; there was no question of that. He had taken her into his home and raised her as his own daughter when her parents died. He had given her a British name, so long ago that she had forgotten her Roman one (although she knew her family name had been Colatinus). Cador deserved her complete obedience. Besides, there was no alternative.

'I don't want to marry an old man,' she whispered to

Con, as they finished their mock-fight.

He looked at her bright eyes and flushed cheeks and sighed. 'Ambrosius is a noble man, Mara. A woman should be proud to be his wife.'

'She *should* be,' answered Mara, tidying her hair, 'and if it has to be me then I *shall* be proud. But that's not the same as wanting to marry a man, is it?'

'Still, you said yourself it was only a rumour,' said Con.

It was Mara's turn to sigh. Ambrosius Aurelius was a noble man indeed. Everyone in Cornwall knew what a fine general he was. Last of the Romans, people called him. He had pushed back the Saxons in many fierce battles. In these dark times when everyone feared the Saxon raiders, Ambrosius was the one name to put a smile on every face and hope in every heart.

But Mara had seen him. And he was an old man of at least forty winters. She was only thirteen and she had seen nothing of the world outside Cador's hall. It was all because she had had the misfortune to be born female.

'You promised to help me,' she repeated to her foster-brother. 'It's my one chance to see a bit of life before I have to take up my distaff and become a respectable married lady.'

And Con, laughing, yielded to her.

The small band of warriors pitched camp and set their horses to graze before foraging for firewood. Their leader, a strongly-built man with a red beard, was strikingly different from his shorter, dark-haired fighting men. He sat, exhausted, with his back against a tree and stretched his long legs to the fire. One of his men, Cei, came back with a couple of rabbits for the pot, and soon the smell of a stew, combined with the woodsmoke, scented the late afternoon air. The leader slept.

He was rudely awakened by shouting. Two of his men were holding a boy who was struggling to escape.

'What's this?' demanded the red-bearded man.

'A Saxon spy,' replied one of the warriors. 'We caught him sneaking round the camp. He'll be back off to his masters with news of our position if we let him go.'

'I'm not a Saxon,' said the boy furiously and spat.

'Look at the colour of him,' said Cei. 'He's too fair and ruddy to be a Briton.'

The boy stared boldly at the leader. 'What about him?' he panted. 'Is he a Saxon with his red hair and beard?'

Cei slapped the boy hard across the cheek, bringing a more fiery colour to his skin. But his leader stopped him from landing another blow.

'I am Artognou,' he said to the boy. 'And no Saxon.

I'm a Briton of Roman family and second-in-command to Ambrosius.'

The boy said nothing.

'You know my name and title, boy,' said Artognou, not unkindly. 'Now you must tell me yours – and what you were doing spying on my camp.'

'Not spying,' said the boy sulkily. 'I was just out with my dogs, looking for rabbits, when your men grabbed me. I didn't even know you were here.'

'Where do you come from?' asked Artognou.

The boy pointed down the valley. 'From the hall of Duke Cador,' he said. 'I'm… I'm one of his serfs. My name is Kern.'

'One of his serfs?' said Artognou, thoughtfully. He took a fold of the boy's tunic between his fingers and felt the cloth. 'Mmm. That's interesting. I'm on my way to see Duke Cador as it happens. We'll take you back.'

He motioned to his men to release their grip on the boy. The boy shook himself free of their grasp and glared at the leader.

'Just let me go. I can find my own way back.'

'I'm sure you can,' said Artognou, calmly. 'But it's dangerous. There are Saxons about, even if you are not one of them. I'm expecting a much larger force of

Ambrosius's men to join me here. We hope to quarter ourselves on Duke Cador while we prepare to fight the invaders. It wouldn't do to lose one of his... serfs for him, even an insignificant boy. Sit down and sup with us.'

The boy looked round as if he would escape but Artognou's men stood in a grinning circle around him. All had knives in their belts and some had long swords too. He subsided in a sulky heap near the fire, pulling his cap low over his brow.

Now that they no longer thought he was a spy, Artognou and his men seemed to ignore the boy, talking about the coming battle. He listened, entranced in spite of himself, to words of the vast Saxon force that was expected. Hundreds of men would come pouring into Summerset. When Artognou's men had all gathered in Cornwall, they would set out to confront them. It wasn't clear if Ambrosius himself would lead the attack.

The boy leaned forward, his eyes shining. This was adventure indeed, to be sitting among soldiers, listening to battle plans. Then he thought what might happen when they took him back to Duke Cador, and squirmed.

'What is it, boy?' asked Artognou. 'Would you like to join us? I could do with a page to look after my horse and see to provender. Would Cador let Kern the serf follow at my heel?'

'Perhaps we needn't ask him?' said the boy and set up a roar of laughter among the men.

There was a great bustle in Cador's hall when the arrival of Artognou and his men was announced. In the commotion, Cei took his eye off Kern for a moment and the boy slipped away. Cei swore.

'Let him go,' said Artognou. 'I warrant we'll see him again. He had the light of battle in his eye.'

Cador was honoured to give lodging to Ambrosius's right-hand man. He spent a lot of time closeted with him, to Constantine's annoyance.

'I'd like to hear his stories myself,' he complained to his foster-sister, who was oddly quiet during Artognou's visit. 'And I'd like to go with him to the battle.'

She looked up sharply then. 'Do you think Father would let you?'

'I don't see why not. I'm old enough to fight and I have to learn some time.'

Ambrosius himself came with news of the Saxons. Rumours reached even to the women's quarters, but they were no longer of marriage. 'They say there's a whole horde of them in Summerset,' said a serving woman. 'Hundreds of the murdering villains. And they do say that Ambrosius isn't going to lead the Britons this time. That he's going to give the job to that young second-in-command of his that's been eating us out of home and hearth these three weeks.'

And so it was. For when the battle force had mustered, Ambrosius came out to bid them farewell and he was without weapons. Artognou led the fighting men, and far back in his train was Constantine, son of Cador. Even further back and on foot was the boy known as Kern, but he was keeping well out of sight.

The men journeyed north-east for many days, into Summerset. Their scouts came back with more and more alarming news of the numbers of Saxons. Every man in the much smaller British army looked grim at the news. And every man knew he would be lucky to survive the coming conflict.

Both sides grew near to an even stretch of land under a grassy hill. Here the Britons camped for what they knew must be the last night before the battle. Kern brought Artognou his meat but the leader gave him no acknowledgement. He had shown no surprise when the serf had shown up in his train.

Pages and other servants were not allowed in the battle. Kern had to stay behind next morning when the grim-faced Britons set off to fight. And it was worse than he had ever imagined. The sounds of the battle went on all day and late into the evening. The terrible cries of men and horses wounded and dying. Kern sat all day screwed into a tight ball with his hands over his ears. He was not only horrified but deathly scared. What would the Saxons do to an abandoned British camp with its stragglers and servants?

Towards nightfall, men began to stagger back to camp. They were so covered in blood and bore such awful wounds that Kern was sure the Saxons had been victorious.

But they weren't fleeing. Gradually as men called for water and warm food, Kern came out of his daze and realised that there were cheerful shouts amid the groans. The Saxons hadn't won!

Kern recognised Cei although his face was caked in blood and his clothes mudstained. 'Bring me mead, boy!' he yelled. 'We must have something to drink Artognou's health!'

'Did we win?' asked Kern.

'Did we win?' laughed Cei. 'Boy, we have won the greatest victory in the history of this island. Artognou is a hero! He slaughtered hundreds of Saxons with his own hand. There has never been a leader like him.'

There was great rejoicing at Cador's hall when Constantine returned. His arm was in a sling and he had a livid scar on his cheek but he was happy. And he had brought Artognou with him.

The hero clasped arms with his host Cador and went in to meet Ambrosius, who had stayed behind during the battle of Mount Badon. But Cador had a worried look about him in spite of the great victory, and Constantine caught what he thought was his foster-sister's name.

As soon as he could, he sought her out in the women's quarters. But there, all was in an uproar. No, he couldn't speak to her; she was being bathed by her serving woman. But Constantine picked up a sense that she was in terrible disgrace.

That night a great feast was given, which Cador's people had started preparing as soon as messengers had brought news of the Saxon rout. The banquet was served at long tables in the Hall and the successful warriors had wine brought to them by Cador's own womenfolk.

Constantine saw to his relief that his foster-sister was among them. She smiled briefly at him when she poured his wine but there was no time to talk and she seemed very subdued. Constantine noticed that she wouldn't meet Cador's eye and he guessed that she had received a strong rebuke for some misdemeanour.

At the end of the meal, Ambrosius rose to his feet.

'Duke Cador, I have a toast to make. To the fighting men who won the day at Mount Badon.'

The hall erupted with shouts as grinning and happy Britons drank one another's health. When the noise died down, Ambrosius said, 'And I have an announcement to make. Today, I stand down as your general and from now on I appoint Artognou as Dux Bellorum, leader of battles, in my place.'

If the hall had been noisy before, it was now deafening. Ambrosius sat down and Cador rose, somewhat unsteadily.

'I too have an announcement to make, Generals,' he said. 'It concerns my foster-daughter, Guanhumara.'

Constantine looked up quickly. So that was it! Cador had told her that she was to be married and she had tried to refuse the honour. But Mara looked as surprised as he felt.

Cador motioned her to his side. 'I have brought her up as my own since her parents died. Now I am happy to say that she has been sought and given in marriage. Come here, and accept your husband.'

Cador took the girl's hand and led her to Ambrosius. But he went past him, and it was Artognou's hand that grasped hers. Guanhumara flushed to the roots of her red-gold hair and Artognou's men cheered their leader to the roof.

Artognou stood to receive his bride and said, 'I thank Cador for bestowing on me the most precious gift under his roof. I welcome the Lady Guanhumara to be my bride. Not only is she beautiful and of noble birth, but I know she has the spirit to be a good wife to a leader of battles.' And he lifted her hand to his lips and kissed it.

Among the general merriment, Constantine felt a pang of jealousy. But he was relieved for Mara that she didn't have to marry an old man. It was a good marriage for her, and Artognou was a brave warrior. But Constantine wondered if he knew what he was taking on.

She was a determined and wilful girl. Take that business when she had insisted that he lend her some clothes so that she could go roaming round the hillside dressed as a boy. To experience some freedom, she had said. And then he remembered. She had never given him those clothes back.

NOTE

In the summer of 1998 a slate was found at Tintagel in Cornwall bearing the scratched inscription: 'Artognou, father of a descendant of Coll, has made this.' Historians said the name would have been pronounced 'Arthnou' and might provide the first tangible proof of the historical existence of the man we know as King Arthur.

7th
CENTURY

———✶———

ANNIE DALTON

ANGEL TO ANGEL

Illustrated by Tim Stevens

ANNIE DALTON

ANGEL TO ANGEL

When the call came, my old teacher, Miss Rowntree, was giving me an ear-bashing. 'There's more to life than makeovers, Melanie,' she nagged. I tried to tell her dying had totally improved my attitude; that the Agency was so impressed, they were sending me on a trouble-shooting mission! But dreams never work out the way you want them to, and an irritating bell had started to ring.

I woke up and answered the phone.

'We need you right away,' said Michael's voice. 'We've got a hiccup in seventh-century Ireland.'

I peered outside. An Agency limo was waiting, its lights blinking in the dark. 'Omigod!' I squeaked. 'They really are letting me go solo!'

Down at Headquarters, one of the night staff gave my skirt a disbelieving stare. 'Are you sure they didn't confuse her with another agent?' he muttered. I'd thrown on the first clothes I could find. It wasn't my fault they were short and sparkly.

'Sorry for the short notice,' said Michael, whizzing me through Departures. Mike's a sweetie, but totally terrifying like all archangels. He started up about how the Agency wanted me to rescue a valuable saint, from bloodthirsty pagans presumably. But I was in such a flap, I didn't take in the details.

'All our experienced agents are tied up in the late 1990s,' Michael sighed. 'That period is such a drain on our resources.'

Tell me about it. I'm still sore about being permanently removed from history by a speeding joyrider, the day after my thirteenth birthday. Sometimes I worry that they won't ever sort my favourite century out. But Michael's dead confident.

I know what you're thinking. Melanie Beeby, training to be an angel! This is a joke, right? That's what *I* thought. But Orlando (he's another trainee and totally gorgeous!) set me straight. 'The Agency's been going quite a few millennia, Mel. They know angel material when they see it.'

Of course, strictly speaking I'm not Mel any more. Angels travel in time as well as space, you see. And like Michael says, 'You can't have the angel Melanie popping up in ancient Egypt. It confuses people.' So my angel name is Helix. Dignified or what!

Still, it was a hairy moment when the door on my time-portal slid shut. Weird stuff flitted through my head. Like, if Miss Rowntree could only see me now. And what was that sweet-faced boy Orlando up to these days? I hadn't seen him for months. We're not encouraged to discuss each other's comings and goings. The tutors just say, 'He moves in mysterious ways,' which basically means MYOB.

'Erm, what have I got to do in that century again?' I yelled through the glass.

Michael's eyebrows shot up. 'You did memorise your manual?'

Luckily, just then my portal lit up like the Blackpool

illuminations, and I was catapulted into a seventh-century sunrise.

What a trip! I tried to act like Helix, all calm and dignified, but a few Melanie-style squeals *might* have leaked out. Anyway, first I got this like, *huge* overview of the entire British Isles. Wow, was the place empty! Then as I got closer I saw all these brilliant details. Whales coming up for air. Fishermen mending nets. Even a musician on the shore, trying out a cool song on his weird little harp.

Then, next thing, I was tumbling to earth, nose to nose with some tiny violets. Hello, world, I'm back. It's me, Melanie!

I was just admiring the scenery (a hill with bouncy little lambs, plus stream and fluffy pussy-willows) when a chariot thundered past. The driver had the dirtiest hair I've ever seen and more tattoos than the average biker. He hurtled into the distance, his outsized wheels churning up the mud.

Well, can't stand about all day, I thought. Better rescue this wrinkly old saint or whatever.

I headed for a village at the top of the hill. I say 'village', but it was more like a bunch of giant bee-hives really. People were up and about already. Feeding horses, lighting fires; dirty little kids racing round scattering chickens. The usual Robin Hood stuff. This was the place, no question. True, there wasn't a saint in sight. But he was probably tied up nearby. Agency timing is dead reliable like that.

Outside one of the huts, youths were taking turns firing arrows at a straw target, jeering when someone missed. I think they were trying to impress these two girls, but the girls went on eating their dried plums, completely ignoring them.

'King, warrior, shepherd, saint,' chanted the red-headed girl. She counted again but it still came out 'saint'. 'Give me yours, Brigid,' she demanded. 'Or I'll never find a king to buy me a gold chain. A big one I want, mind. Thick enough to choke a donkey!'

'Throw one stone away, Niamh, and marry the shepherd,' teased Brigid.

Niamh laughed. 'And spend my days stinking of damp wool, like Mother!'

'Niamh! Get in here!' yelled a woman's voice.

The girl rolled her eyes. 'We're to clean the wall hangings today.' She scrambled to her feet and I followed her indoors.

You've probably heard angels can read people's

thoughts? The truth is, we can't *not* do it; human thoughts just jump out at us like radio signals. So I found out about Niamh's life with no trouble at all.

For instance, her people *weren't* pagans. So it was highly unlikely they'd got my saint under lock and key somewhere. I found out other things too. Like when Niamh was little, she sang all day long for sheer enjoyment. Until her Mum remarked that no-one in their right mind would marry a girl who cawed like a crow. After that, Niamh gave up on life and took up daydreaming full-time, deciding her only hope was to find a king to marry.

Then a few months ago, walking in the hazel woods, she stumbled across an incredibly beautiful young man, delirious with fever.

Naturally Niamh was primed to recognise royal blood when she saw it. So she came back every day to spoon nettle soup into him, until he was well enough to remember his name, which turned out to be Colum. Of course, Niamh was thrilled when Colum finally confessed his father was the king of Kinvara. Her dream was coming true!

You see, the king wanted his son to be a great warrior but Colum hated violence. That's why he was hiding out in the woods, eating nuts and berries. Niamh promised not to tell a soul she'd seen him.

Colum was nothing like the tough biker-types in Niamh's village. He was so pure and gentle, shy forest creatures came up to lick his hands. Niamh thought this was pretty weird. But he'd probably grow out of it, once he'd resumed his royal responsibilities. So all winter she'd been smuggling him food and clothing, convinced he'd soon forget his silly quarrel and take her home to Kinvara with him.

I found out something else about Niamh as I watched her dreamily doing her chores. When no-one was around, she sang to herself, in a voice which made my whole spine tingle.

Miss Rowntree says TV soaps rot your brains. But I learned heaps from watching them. For instance, I knew right off Niamh didn't love Colum. He was just her most convenient career option. Unfortunately there was one tiny drawback. Me.

You see, by now I'd figured out that Colum was the saint the Agency'd sent me to rescue. Not from bloodthirsty pagans. But from Niamh.

I don't know how clued up you are about the Dark Ages? Well, during that period, it was only a bunch of wild and wonderful Irish saints who kept the divine light burning in Europe. Some of these saints were so holy that natural laws were suspended in their vicinity. Which basically means miracles became, like, normal. And hopefully this balanced out the really gross stuff going on elsewhere. So you can see why the Agency couldn't afford to lose a saint. It'd be like England losing a striker during the World Cup.

But what about Niamh? Okay, she was no saint. But didn't she count for anything? Wasn't there any way I could do this without hurting her feelings?

Anyway, when Niamh sneaked away to the woods that night, I followed. But when we got there, there was a bunch of total strangers in Colum's grove, listening to him explaining about Time being like a honeycomb with many chambers. (I think that was it.)

'Who are these people?' demanded Niamh.

'My friends,' said Colum serenely.

'But you love *me*,' yelled Niamh, her nostrils going pinched and white, which I'm afraid did absolutely nothing for her.

'Colum loves all creation,' said a girl. 'Birds, stones, dew.'

So of course Niamh went crashing off into the woods, furious about wasting her time on some bloke who loved dew. At the same moment Colum moved near the fire. And for the first time I saw his sweet familiar face.

'*Orlando?*' I whispered.

He didn't seem surprised to see me. 'I'm at my wits' end, Mel,' he sighed. 'Niamh's a great kid. But I can't marry her. It would ruin the Agency's strategy.'

'I didn't know angels could be saints,' I said.

'They were one short,' he explained casually. 'I'm helping out.' A baby deer nuzzled his hand. And in the branches over our heads, a couple of owls looked down adoringly. Orlando really made an excellent saint.

'But she'll tell the King you're here,' I said. 'He'll have you killed and Ireland will *still* be a saint short of a full set.'

No-one could hear us, by the way. It was strictly angel to angel.

'That's why I asked the Agency to send you,' said Orlando.

'You're kidding! You actually *asked* for me?'

'Yes. Because you'll know how to help her,' he said simply.

And for a dizzy second I was falling through the sunrise again. And as I fell, I registered once again that young musician practising his song on a lonely beach.

Orlando was right. I knew exactly what to do.

Look, the next bit is dead technical, okay, unless you're into angel science. All you need to know is that with a helpful cosmic nudge or three, they finally met up; Niamh and her travelling musician. (His name was Marvan by the way.) And it turned out they were made for each other. So, mission accomplished, I'd say!

Back at the Agency, Michael gave me a tape of the whole experience, for future reference. But I keep rewinding to the bit where they're on the beach, at sunset, and Marvan finally says the words I'd been whispering to him. 'So Niamh, won't you sing for me?'

And Niamh tosses her head like Scarlett O'Hara in *Gone with the Wind* and says, 'I will not. My mother says I sound like a crow.'

But you'll never guess what Marvan says next, with no help whatsoever.

'Are you telling me there is no song locked inside that lovely swan's throat of yours?'

Romantic or what!! So Niamh sings and Marvan's totally blown away by her beautiful voice, like I knew he would be. Then he tells her how the two of them will travel the wide world, and perform before the High King of Ireland himself. And off they go, hand in hand.

And at that exact moment some wild geese fly overhead. It makes me cry every time. And I just know that Miss Rowntree would totally approve.

So that's all really. Except to say, don't worry, next time I get a midnight call, I'll be properly prepared. It took ages but I've finally come up with the perfect outfit; cropped top, combats and some cool boots. To me this look says committed, it says *now*, it says ready for action.

I mean, I'm an angel, so I should look *divine*, right?

8th
CENTURY

———★———

MELVIN BURGESS

ODIN'S DAY

Illustrated by David Wyatt

MELVIN BURGESS

ODIN'S DAY

It had rained all year. It was still raining now, even though the water was turning to ice. The ground around the temple was a sodden mud bath that leaked freezing water through your boots. A hard, icy surface formed on it each night and if you got up early enough you could slide on it for half an hour or so. That was wild fun. The whole place was full of swirling children and cursing adults trying to do their chores. Then the rain started again, the horses began tramping all around the place and the ice turned briefly into daggers that hurt your hands if you fell. Then it all melted back into one great miry puddle, half a mile across.

This was the third year of famine. The rain had rotted everything it hadn't flattened. Under their furs and rags, young and old were just bags of bones. Everyone was hoping that the festival would bring some relief.

By mid-morning the sacrifices began. The gods – Thor, Odin and Frey – were brought out of the temple into the glade where the beasts stood tethered or caged, anxiously moaning and whining. They were all strong, fat beasts. In this year of famine, their plumpness looked strange, almost as if there was something wrong with them. The sun emerged above the temple, shining white and hard and cold in the pale sky. The dark shapes in the sacred trees glistened with wet in the light and the ravens and crows that strutted up and down the evergreen branches were black with glee. In a time like this, they were the only ones with a feast to go to.

There were seven animals – horse, goat, eagle, raven, wolf, boar and bull. The priests dragged them forward and held them tight with ropes and slashed at their throats with iron swords. There was a violent gush of hot blood splashing on to the stones. The beasts uttered no sound at the blow, but they jumped, or tried to; the ropes caught them short before they left the ground. They sank to their knees, the blood flowed out of them, and they were dead within a minute.

Vili stood with his family, beside himself with excitement. He was waiting to see the wolf die. The wolf was a great tall grey creature, and Vili had been with his brothers when they had captured him. They had had to hold the dogs off while he fought like a giant in the net, and two of the men had been bitten trying to get him out. Then he had been a scraggy, bony beast, but now, after a month of feeding, he was fat and glossy, and angrier than ever.

It took four men to hold the iron-grey animal still and draw his head up. Smelling the blood, he roared in his bonds. His growls stopped short when his throat was cut.

'Does Odin question the dead wolf too?' Vili asked a man standing by him.

The man, a grizzled old soldier who owned a longhouse some ten miles east of Vili's father's hall, scratched his head. 'Some of them must go to Valhalla to hunt, but I never heard of a wolf in Hel or Niflhel,' he said at last.

Someone else leant across. 'I think they must learn something when they die. Why else would we hang them up?'

Vili wrinkled his nose, then shuddered. What secrets did the dead tell? He looked at the grey wolf, limp and disgusting now that he was dead, dumped on the cart with the other dead animals. Could Odin really make him talk without even bringing him back to life? How would he act? And most of all... what would his voice sound like, all the way from Hel?

He stayed restlessly to watch the other creatures, especially the bull, a huge beast who knew what was coming. It took twelve men to hold him still as the sword ended his days, and he bled like a river. But it was the end that really fascinated and scared the boy, when the highest of all sacrifices was made. This one did not need to be dragged – he came on his own. Thor and Frey liked goats and boars, but Odin demanded a human life.

A man stepped forward and the crowd moved closer, cutting off Vili's view. He squeaked and pulled on his brother's sleeve, but Vali scowled and shook his head and wouldn't lift him up, so the youngster had to push his way forward. Then he was sorry he had, because the man turned his head and looked full on him for a second. The boy pulled back and hid, scared that the man would remember when he was dead that Vili had come to watch him die.

The sacrifices were always held here in the open, among the sacred trees that grew around the temple. The temple itself was splendid, with gold and silver bands and a great chain interwoven around the gates. Every day for nine days, the stone idols of Odin, Thor and Frey had been taken out to see the blood spilt. Every day for nine days, eight living creatures were killed for them. Those chosen for the gods were always the best of their race… strong, fierce and young. The Uppsala Festival was held only once every nine years, and it was important this time especially that it went well. The famine was dreadful. Men and beasts were dying in their hundreds and sacrifice was the only way to ask the gods to help.

Afterwards, the bodies were hung in the trees. With this latest batch on the eighth day, there would be sixty-four dead things hanging like strange giant fruit from the evergreen branches of the sacred grove. Tomorrow, there would be seventy-two, a holy number; and the festival would be over.

Vili of course was there to watch with his brothers and sisters, his father and mother. He was fascinated by the sight of these once quick creatures hauled up into the sky. At night, Odin, the god of mysteries, would come with his terrifying runes and question them. What would he ask? What would they answer? Most people regarded Thor as the greatest of the gods. He was the one who protected the world. But Vili's father was a King, and Kings worshipped Odin.

Up in the trees, men were fixing ropes to haul the beasts up. Some, like the goats and the wolves, could be winched up quite easily. Others, like the bull, took a team of strong men to get them into the sky. The leaves shook, the branches groaned, and the great animals rose slowly, impossibly, offered into the hands of the gods. Seven horses, seven boars, seven bulls; the trees were clustered with these giants bending the branches. There were no foals or calves; these were all full-grown stallions, bulls and boars. Seven eagles and seven ravens dripped blood from their beaks. Seven goats and seven wolves stared blindly down at the ground. Seven men twisted slowly on their ropes.

Vili stared up and gulped. He could understand the sacrifice only too well: men had to kill to live, why not the gods? But the thought of Odin creeping out in his broad hat and his cloak to make these still, senseless things talk made him tremble with fear... and with longing. Yes... he wanted to know the secrets of the dead too. He had even considered hiding near these gibbet trees to hear what they said when Odin made them talk. So far, he hadn't dared to do it.

As he watched the dead men twisting in the leaves, Vili asked his father, 'Do they mind dying for Odin?'

Vikar took his hand. 'It's a great honour. He's gone to Odin. He's gone to Odin,' he said. Vili could feel his father's cold hand trembling in his, but he did not understand what it meant.

The sacrifices were terrible, but that wasn't all there was to it. The gods enjoyed life to the full, and they expected people to as well. In the evening there were fires and eating and drinking, music and songs. People had not much energy to spare, but they gave what they had to the festival. For a few hours the fields and woods around the temple were ablaze with fires and full of the smells of food, as if this was a year of plenty. The mud steamed and baked at the edges of the flames, goats and wildfowl sputtered on spits. The skalds sang songs of the gods and of the great and famous, past and present – Volsung and his twelve sons, Sigurd and the dragon.

And they sang songs of Vikar. Vili's father had ruled his kingdom for only eight years, three of them in famine, but he had fed his people by raiding the neighbouring kingdoms. He was a warrior, a hero. And yet the gods had not lifted the famine, even for him. That night Vili heard three poets in different parts of the field sing his father's praises, and he went to bed feeling every inch the son of a king.

The festivities did not last long. As the fires burned, a deadly wind began to blow. The clouds vanished, the stars shone like stones, and a thick layers of hoar frost began to form on the dead ones hanging in the grove. The people turned their faces into the wind and felt the ice bite deep. Already the mud was hard with ice, despite the fires. No one was in a mood to stay up late. They left swiftly for their tents. Soon the fields and woods were left to the sky, to the frost, and to Odin.

This would be an end to the rain; even your blood would freeze on a night like this. The beasts turned solid in the trees, the mud hardened inch by inch, deeper and deeper into the ground. The creatures in their hideaways, the people in theirs — all kept their warmth huddled up close. In Vikar's tent though, his wife and older daughters and sons stayed up late to be with their father. When at last he went to bed, the king was unable to sleep. His wife lay by his side and let the tears trace silently down her face. He stroked her cheeks and said nothing when he felt the wet. What was there to say?

Out in the frosty night a fox trotted across the ice-crusted mud to the gibbet trees, attracted by the smell. She came right up beneath the branches and looked up at the great fruits of meat glistening softly with frost in the white moonlight. It was all far out of the reach of the little vixen, who yawned widely and carried on her way over the still fields, to sniff around the glowing embers for forgotten bones.

As the fox made her way across the frozen mud another small figure emerged from one of the hide tents. Vili, heartened by the songs he had heard that evening, had decided that tonight he would visit the gibbet and try to see Odin. He was the son of a king, a hero! Nothing should scare him…

He *was* scared, though. He was terrified. The night was so still, the air was so full of ice. He could see the darkness of the trees in the moonlight, and the dark, heavy shapes of the stallions and bulls hanging there. Even so, he wrapped his furs close around him and began to slip his feet – one, two, one, two – over the icy mud.

And then the night was broken by a terrifying voice. It split the still air and shattered the night. It went on and on and on – some great creature groaning, groaning in pain...

Vili caught sight of the little vixen out of the corner of his eye, literally jumping a yard into the air before she made off across the frozen mud like a hare. He screamed and tried to run, but fell at once on to the spear-sharp ridges of ice. Still the thing was groaning! It must be a bull! Or a horse! Or a dead man...?

Picking himself up, he half-ran, half-crawled, half-skated back to his tent, dived through the flaps and cringed in terror inside. How had he been so stupid as to think he was brave enough to watch Odin talking to the dead?

Outside, the groans died down. For a while nothing moved, and then some warriors pulled on their clothes and went to see what was happening.

As Vili thought, it had been a bull, but not his voice. Ice had formed in the crook where the branch bearing his weight joined to the trunk. Melting and re-freezing again at night, this frozen wedge had levered a crack in the wood and the beast's huge weight had done the rest. Splitting, the tree had lowered the bull gently to the ground and had groaned like a man as it did it.

The men stared anxiously at the great hard beast lying awkwardly on the frost. It confirmed one thing to them: on the last day they must make the highest of all sacrifices to Odin, in the hope that he would find a way to end this terrible long night of rain and ice that had gripped the land for so many years.

The next morning Vili was quiet, shaken by the events of the night before. At last he seemed to be aware that something terrible was going to happen, although he had no idea what. He watched his father dress himself in his finest clothes, with his best weapons and jewels – his golden pins and arm bands, his cloak, his sword decorated with three-coloured gold. He was so proud to see his father in all his glory, but still, even as they made their way to the temple, he had no idea. He watched the animals killed without thinking. There were two bulls this morning, since one had been refused. When the last animal had been killed and it was time for the man, Vili stared for long seconds as his father stepped forward towards the gods. Then, as he finally realised, he cried out suddenly in the quietness…

'No!'

His father turned to look him full in the face, just as the last one had. 'I am the best of all,' he said proudly. 'Odin will lift this ice for me.'

Then he stepped forward and lifted his sword as a ring of priests closed in. When a king was given to Odin, he died fighting.

9th
CENTURY

——————— ✶ ———————

GILLIAN CROSS

BROTHER AELRED'S FEET

Illustrated by Tim Stevens

GILLIAN CROSS

BROTHER AELRED'S FEET

If Brother Aelred stepped into the dairy, the milk turned sour. If he helped in the kitchen, the meat went rotten. If he walked through the vegetable garden, next day's soup tasted of old socks.

Aelred had the smelliest feet in the whole ninth century. Anywhere. And he was the only person who couldn't smell them.

Apart from that, he was an ideal monk. He was plump and humble and very short, but he could sing like an angel. And when he copied manuscripts, he filled them with tiny, beautiful pictures. If it hadn't been for his feet…

But his feet were impossible.

At last, the old Abbot had an idea. He called Aelred into his cell. 'Brother,' he said, 'I have a job for you.'

Aelred beamed. 'In the scriptorium, Father? Copying the holy books?'

The Abbot thought of Aelred's beautiful manuscripts. Then he thought of the cramped, airless room where the monks sat copying out the gospels and the service books.

'Not the scriptorium,' he said gently.

Aelred's face fell. Then he brightened. 'What about the choir? I love singing psalms in St Meregonda's chapel.'

The Abbot remembered Aelred's fine tenor voice. But he also remembered the tiny, windowless chapel where St Meregonda's relics lay. 'I was thinking of a more open-air job,' he said. 'How do you feel about – pigs?'

'*Pigs?*'

The monastery pigs were wild and hairy and ugly. But Aelred was a humble man. He knelt and kissed the Abbot's ring.

'Thank you, Father,' he said. 'I'll take good care of the pigs.'

And he did. Every morning, he drove them up the hill behind the monastery. He stayed there all day, praying and singing psalms and canticles, while the pigs grunted and rooted for acorns.

The pigs didn't mind Aelred's feet. In fact, they rather liked the smell. They liked his singing, too. And they loved Aelred himself, because he looked after them so well.

When he had finished singing, Aelred collected pieces of bark and decorated them with pictures of St Meregonda, colouring them with berries and leaves and roots.

That was what he was doing when the Danes came. He had just finished drawing St Meregonda's dragon when he glimpsed something fluttering in the bay beyond the hill. Looking down, he saw a longship anchored off the shore. Huge warriors were leaping out of it, with battleaxes in their hands.

Aelred didn't waste a second. Tucking the bark picture into his belt, he race down to the monastery, shouting at the top of his voice.

'Northmen! Northmen!'

The pigs followed him, squealing shrilly, and they all crashed through the front gate of the monastery.

'Northmen!' Aelred yelled. 'The Northmen have landed in the bay!'

All the other monks came hurrying out of their cells. Their faces were white. They knew how the Danes smashed and looted and pillaged.

Only the Abbot was calm. 'We can hide in the forest,' he said. 'But we must save our treasures. Who will take them across the causeway to the mainland?'

There was a terrible, terrified silence. Even the pigs stopped oinking.

The Abbot frowned. 'We can't let the Danes capture our holy books and the relics of St Meregonda. Will no one save them?'

Aelred stepped forward. 'I will,' he said.

Aelred? No one could believe it. He was much too small to fight off any Danes.

But the old Abbot smiled at him. 'God gives us all different gifts. Maybe he will use yours now, Brother Aelred. Let us hurry.'

Monks raced off in all directions, tripping over the pigs as they went. Out came the big wooden chest from the church. St Meregonda's relics and the holy books were packed into it and it was lifted on to the monastery's donkey cart.

When the pigs saw Aelred leaving with the cart, they tried to follow him, but the monks drove them back and shut them into the barn. They grunted miserably as they heard Aelred and the donkey marching away.

He was just out of sight when the Danes came howling over the hill, brandishing axes and bellowing threats. The monks took one look and raced into the forest. By the time the Danes reached the monastery, it was deserted.

The Danish leader was a wild giant of a man called Erik. He smashed down the monastery gate and charged in, shouting at his men.

'ATTACK!'

They followed, with their axes waving, but there was no one to attack. Erik glared round.

'LOOT AND PILLAGE!' he yelled.

The Danes ransacked the monastery buildings. There were no treasures. No monks. But when they opened the barn doors, out galloped a herd of wild, hairy pigs, snorting angrily.

Erik hadn't been expecting pigs. He had seventeen brothers, all bigger and fiercer than he was, and he wanted some rare and precious treasure, to impress them. But pigs were better than nothing.

'SEIZE THEM!' he bellowed.

The Danes tried, but the pigs had different ideas. They dodged and doubled and darted, heading for the gate. They didn't want to be seized. They wanted to follow Aelred.

'AFTER THEM!' raged Erik.

Down the road streamed the pigs, squealing and grunting, with the Danes pelting in chase. Aelred was safely out of sight, but the pigs knew exactly where he'd gone. They charged after him.

And the Danes followed them.

A mile ahead, Aelred heard the noise and he was terrified. He didn't know what was going on, but he tugged at the donkey's bridle, trying to make it go faster. That was a mistake. The donkey planted its feet firmly in the mud and refused to move.

Aelred wanted to run, but he couldn't leave the holy relics and the precious books. And the wooden chest was too heavy to move. In desperation, he opened the lid and squeezed inside the chest himself. Pulling the lid down, he lay as still as he could.

It wasn't a great plan. When the pigs eventually

reached the cart, they crowded joyfully round it, oinking at the chest. The Danes thundered up behind and Erik's eyes gleamed. His instinct told him that there was something very special inside that chest.

The kind of thing he needed to impress his brothers.

'PILLAGE!' he yelled.

Two massive Danes leaped forward and began to tug at the lid of the chest. The others crowded round, eager to see what treasures were inside. Wedged in between the books and the relics, Aelred clutched desperately at the rim of the lid, holding it shut.

But he didn't stand a chance. More and more Danes grabbed it, heaving hard.

'GET IT OPEN, YOU WEAKLINGS!' Erik was bellowing.

The Danes tugged until their faces went purple, and Aelred's fingers slipped and lost their grip. With a crash, the lid of the box flew open...

... and out flooded the smell of Aelred's feet.

They'd been shut inside the chest for almost half an hour. The smell was ripe and rich and concentrated and it hit the Danes full on. They staggered backwards, swayed dizzily – and passed out.

Cautiously, Aelred sat up and looked round. What

was going on? He was surrounded by unconscious Danes and wild, hairy pigs.

When the pigs saw him, they went berserk with joy. Oinking and squealing, they charged up to him, pushing their snouts against his robe and chewing his fingers.

'Peace,' said Aelred.

But the pigs were too excited to stop. The squealing got louder and louder. Aelred did the only thing he knew that calmed them down.

He started to sing.

He was still singing when the Danes opened their eyes. One by one, they sat up and looked round, wondering who'd knocked them out. They were expecting to see a giant or an army of English soldiers. But there was no one there except a little fat monk sitting in a wooden box, singing like an angel. All round the box were wild, hairy pigs, gazing up adoringly at him.

The Danes were terrified. They thought Aelred was a wizard.

Erik was the last man to come round. He had been nearest to the chest and caught the full blast of Aelred's feet. He didn't remember exactly what had happened because he'd hit his head on the ground, but he could see there was something extraordinary going on. He was

amazed to find himself trembling.

'WHO ARE YOU?' he yelled at Aelred.

Aelred didn't understand the language of the Danes, but he saw that Erik was confused and afraid.

'Peace,' he said soothingly. Exactly as he said it to the pigs. He felt silly sitting in the box, so he started to climb out, singing gently. He sang the pigs' favourite song.

'*Pa-a-ax vo-bi-is-cum.*'

Erik was even more afraid. He thought it was a spell. Jumping up, he seized his axe, ready to chop Aelred into pieces if he came any closer. All the other Danes watched in terror. They were convinced that Aelred was a magician and they were sure he would blast them with lightning if Erik attacked him. But they were frightened of Erik as well. They didn't know what to do.

'*Pa-a-ax vo-bi-is-cum,*' sang Aelred soothingly, jumping down from the cart. Up went Erik's axe, ready for the death blow.

But at the last moment, just before the axe fell, something flapped at Aelred's waist. A piece of bark tucked into his belt. Erik glimpsed lines and marks on it, and he stepped back.

'MAGIC!' he shouted.

Aelred didn't understand, but he saw Erik looking at

the bark. 'Peace,' he said again. Smiling, he pulled the bark from his belt and held it out.

Erik reached out nervously and took it. Looking down, he saw a small, bright picture of a woman leading a ferocious dragon. He didn't know anything about St Meregonda, so he was certain that the bark was a magic charm. A rare and precious treasure to impress his seventeen brothers. He knelt down and bowed to Aelred.

It's always sensible to keep on good terms with magicians.

Then he leapt up and started giving orders. To Aelred's amazement, the other Danes all bowed too. Then they began to march away up the road, singing Aelred's song.

'*Pa-a-ax vob-i-is-cum...*'

Aelred waited for a long time, until the sound of singing had died away completely. Then he picked up the donkey's bridle and began to lead it back to the monastery, with the pigs trotting along behind.

The other monks had come out of hiding. They were standing at the top of the hill, watching the Danish longship sail away. When they saw Aelred, they ran down the hill to meet him.

'Well done, Brother!' said the Abbot. 'The Danes

came to loot and pillage, but you have sent them away singing about peace.'

Aelred was baffled. 'What did *I* do?'

The monks couldn't tell him, but they stood and cheered. Then they led him into the church, for a service of thanksgiving. Afterwards, the Abbot took him aside.

'You deserve a reward, Brother,' he said. 'Would you like to work in the scriptorium?'

Aelred thought about it. Then he thought about the pigs.

'Thank you, Father,' he said. 'I can't leave the pigs. But I should like to work in the scriptorium in the winter, when it's too dark to go into the woods.'

So that is what he did. In summer, he looked after the pigs, and in winter he copied manuscripts, drawing lovely, intricate pictures in the margins of the holy books.

After a while, the other monks began to notice how pleasant the scriptorium smelt in winter. 'Like incense and roses,' they said.

It took them a long time to realise that it was the smell of Brother Aelred's feet...

10th
CENTURY

— ★ —

ALAN DURANT

THE HAMMER AND THE CROSS

Illustrated by Mark Robertson

ALAN DURANT

THE HAMMER AND THE CROSS

It was a night black as a raven's wing, the wind's bite
sharp as a wolf's tooth. Thunder rumbled and cracked as
though the great god Thor were pounding his mighty
hammer, Mjollnir, against the heavens. Lightning forked
the sky.

A small band of Vikings with their bound captive
struggled across the dark fields. The young Norsemen
were weary and lost, and one had wounds that needed
attention. They sought shelter, but the treeless and

hostile Orcadian landscape held no shelter, it seemed.

The mound was unexpected. A huge grassy dome that rose out of the landscape like the breast of a giantess. Even so, they might have passed by had the lightning not, in glittering fury, revealed an entrance disturbed by the storm.

In a matter of moments the Norsemen had heaved away the stone that obstructed the opening and, stooping, entered the low tunnel they found beyond. Sigurd led, his huge frame almost filling the passageway, his heart flaring with exhilaration at the prospect of treasure – for what else, he thought, could be so closely concealed? His kinsman Harald followed, clutching his bleeding side, young Egil behind him and then their monk captive, with Erlend at the rear.

The Norsemen belonged to Erik Blood-Axe's *lid*, his personal retinue of warriors. They were among a raiding party of thirty who had sailed from York to the Orkney Islands in search of plunder. They had found it too, attacking a monastery near the coast, and looting a rich hoard. But it had not been as easy as they had expected, for the monks had put up a stubborn resistance, many taking up arms to defend their home and treasures. Most had been killed, but there were some Vikings also for whom morning would never come. Dying like true Viking warriors, sword in hand, they would take their seats in Valhalla, the hall of the slain.

The tunnel opened out into a dark chamber. Taking the strike-a-light he wore on a chain around his neck, Sigurd struck a flint to ignite one of the torches they had seized from the monastery – and which had long since extinguished in the fierce wind. In the sudden flame, shadows leapt and skittered like frightened stallions around the solid stone walls. Glancing down, Egil caught his breath. The floor was strewn with bones – human bones. They were not in a chamber of treasure, but of death.

Sigurd was not pleased. He picked up a bone and hurled it across the chamber.

'Bones!' he rasped, as the bone splintered against the opposite wall. 'What use are bones?'

His angry violence, as ever, made Egil uneasy, but it was not he who spoke – it was Erlend. 'Go easy, Sigurd,' he urged, pulling warily at his coarse yellow beard. 'This is a holy place. Who knows what god's powers you may provoke.'

Sigurd laughed harshly. 'Bah! Odin is our god,' he proclaimed, throwing wide his broad, muscle-bound arms. 'He will protect us. All other gods bow before him.' He picked up another bone and held it out to Egil. 'Here, cousin,' he smirked, 'make yourself a new flute. It will surely sound better than that old sheep's bone you blow through.'

Egil pursed his lips and frowned, which made Sigurd laugh again, before tossing the bone aside as if to some waiting hound at table.

They had no wood to light a fire, so had to make themselves as warm as they could with their animal skins. They had food – bread, salted meat and fruit – and a flask of mead that they had taken from the monastery. It was morning since they had last eaten and they fell on the food eagerly, sharing it among the four of them. Sitting alone on the other side of the chamber, their silent captive went hungry.

'You've no need of food,' Sigurd taunted the monk, tearing at a joint of meat with his knife, 'for you'll soon be feeding the wolves yourself.'

The monk stared back at Sigurd, but his face showed no expression. Egil wondered at that. The man could not understand Sigurd's words, of course, but there could be no mistaking the threat in the warrior's voice and demeanour. Yet the young monk's eyes betrayed no fear.

They were striking eyes too, thought Egil – light icy blue, like his own, and deep as the ocean.

After they had eaten, Erlend tended Harald's wound, making a rough poultice with some herbs that he carried and then tearing cloth to bandage it. The gash had appeared bad at first, but now the bleeding had stopped and Harald's life, it seemed, was not in danger. He was obviously in great pain, however. To try to take his mind off his discomfort, Erlend suggested they play a game of *hnefatall*. He scratched a board in the earth with his knife, carefully marking out the squares. For counters, he broke scraps of bone. Erlend, it was agreed, would defend the king from Harald's greater attacking force. Sigurd meanwhile examined his hoard, the prize of which was a silver jewel-encrusted chalice. He fingered it with greedy pleasure.

Egil watched his cousin a moment, then he took out his flute and began to play. The flute had been a present from his father, who had carved and scored it with his own hands. He had given it to Egil on the day he had departed on his last voyage, a trip to the East, to Serkland, from which he had never returned. That had been two winters since. Last winter, Egil's mother, Ingibiorg, had died too. It was then that Sigurd had taken Egil under his wing.

Sigurd was nearly ten years older than Egil and, though cousins, the two were chalk and cheese. Sigurd was a follower of Odin, god of war. He wore the bearskin shirt of a beserker, the wildest, most feared Viking warrior of all. In battle, he was fearless, throwing himself into the thick of the fighting like a man possessed, paying no heed to his own fate or the fate of any other. In the attack on the monastery, he had been at the head of the strike, flailing with two hands his long sword like a giant scythe as he chopped and slashed, severing limbs, slicing through flesh. Egil had witnessed him behead one of the monks with a single savage blow that had turned his stomach.

He, Egil, had taken no part in the slaughter. Yet he had observed all. He was still considered too young to fight, though the time was fast approaching when he too would be expected to wield a sword, axe or spear in battle. The thought sickened him. He was a poet, a singer – his desire was not to be a warrior but a *skald*, a poet fit to entertain a chieftain or a king, like his illustrious namesake, the Icelander Egil Skellagrimsson, the greatest skaldic poet of all.

Already young Egil's prowess as a word-smith and

rune-carver had impressed Erik Blood-Axe, who loved nothing better than to hear his heroic battle feats praised in verse. Though was this really, Egil wondered, the kind of verse he wished to compose? No doubt, Sigurd would expect him to write something in celebration of this latest 'triumph'. But in Egil's eyes the sacking of the monastery had been far from triumphant; it had been bloody butchery, ending up in confusion. Sigurd's reckless pursuit of treasure had been responsible for the division of the raiding party and was the reason why the four Vikings found themselves in this sombre burial dome, waiting for the storm to break and the first glimmer of daylight when they could make their way back to their ship and safety.

Taking the monk captive had been Erlend's idea. In this hostile land, it might be useful to have a hostage he had suggested, staying Sigurd, who had been poised to slay the man as he knelt in prayer. It was only that, though – a stay of execution – as Sigurd stated now, filling his drinking horn once more with mead. 'Tomorrow, you die,' he growled, glowering at his captive with savage resolution. 'At dawn's light, you shall die the death of the blood eagle.'

At these words, the flute slipped from Egil's lips in

alarm. 'Surely there is no need for that, cousin,' he dared to venture. The blood eagle was a horrific, brutal act. The victim's ribcage was hacked through either side of the spine and then his lungs were torn out. It was a cruel and terrible death.

'These people must be taught a lesson,' snarled Sigurd, his dark eyes clouding with the mead. 'Next time they will not be so eager to stand against us. I shall do the blood eagle and then leave his body for the cranes and wolves to devour.'

'But, cousin,' Egil persisted, 'surely the monk would be of more worth alive. Think of the money you might get for such a slave. Isn't that so, Erlend?' he appealed to Sigurd's cooler-headed companion. But Erlend barely looked up from his game.

'Sigurd is right,' he muttered grimly. 'The monk must die. The deaths of our brothers must be avenged. It is our *felag* duty.'

'B-but—' Egil stammered.

'Enough!' Sigurd roared, the mead taking full effect now. 'He dies in the morning.' His eyes had taken on the trance-like, frenzied look they often wore before battle. 'Now we warriors must sleep,' he slurred. 'You shall keep watch.' He thrust his battleaxe at Egil. 'Take this,

Egil Egilsson,' he commanded. 'It is time you became a man.'

As soon as Sigurd had closed his eyes, Egil put down the heavy axe. He peered across at the monk, whose head was bowed now as if in sleep. What danger could he possibly be, poor man? Egil thought.

He had seen monks in his own land, preaching the word of their God, talking of Jesus Christ, who had died on a cross to save the world. They spoke very persuasively and conversions were not uncommon. He had heard it said that in Denmark, King Harald Bluetooth was close to declaring himself for the new faith and banishing the Norse gods to oblivion. It seemed only a matter of time before Norway too bowed to this Christ. It was largely on account of this that Sigurd had decided to leave his homeland and seek out Erik Blood-Axe. In his court at least, declared Sigurd, Odin, Thor and their fellow gods still reigned.

Yet one day even they would die, according to legend; when Ragnarok came, the doom of the gods, they would be destroyed by monsters and giants. Well, perhaps that day had come, Egil reflected. Not as predicted in an orgy of blood and destruction, but in a becalming peace, the death blow delivered not by monstrous beings but by men like this silent monk opposite him who were willing to sacrifice all for their god. He thought again of what Sigurd would do to the man the following day and it made him shiver. As he sat in that cold burial place of a people from some former time who had worshipped other gods, he was overwhelmed by a sense of things passing, ending, dying.

It had been a long and exhausting day and his eyes were drooping. Outside the gale continued, moaning and ululating like a wounded wild beast. To keep himself awake and also to divert his thoughts from their gloomy path, Egil began to scratch out rune-writing on the chamber wall beside him. Meticulously he stroked a verse in praise of his father and mother; then he carved a dragon and recorded beneath it the names of the four Norsemen sheltering in the domed chamber that night. He ended with a boastful flourish, in imitation of the man who had taught him the rune language, Hakaan the Red: *These runes were carved by Egil Egilsson*, he wrote, *the most skilled rune carver on the Western Ocean.*

It was as he put the finishing strokes to this epitaph that the monk spoke.

'You write well, Egil Egilsson,' he said, speaking fluently the Norse tongue, 'but do you not think perhaps you exaggerate your gifts a little?'

Astonished, Egil dropped his knife. Then, flustered, he grabbed at the battleaxe Sigurd had given him and held it up before his frowning face.

The monk smiled. 'You need have no fear of me, Egil,' he said softly. 'I mean you no harm.' He glanced down at his bound hands and feet. 'Besides, as you see, I am well restrained.'

Egil lowered the axe, but his eyes were still wary and startled. 'You speak our language,' he murmured, perplexed. 'Who are you?'

'I am just a humble monk,' the captive replied. 'My name is Ansgar. My father was a Norseman like you and your companions. My mother was a Celt. I was born in this land and have lived here all my life.' His gaze lowered momentarily. 'Now I shall die here too.'

His eyes were raised again now and Egil remarked once more their striking quality, icy-blue like the waters of a fjord. He should have recognised in them at once a fellow Norseman.

'You should have fled when you had the opportunity,' Egil said. Then, curious, he added, 'Why did you not fight like the other monks?'

'I am a man of God, not war, Egil Egilsson,' the

monk answered simply. 'I did not enter the monastery to take up arms, but to worship my Lord Jesus Christ. It is His way – the way of peace – I follow.'

Egil laid down the battleaxe on the earth floor in front of him. 'I shall tell Sigurd,' he said. 'He will not kill a fellow Norseman…'

'No, Egil,' said the monk with sudden urgency. 'It will make no difference. Your cousin will kill me whatever. He is Odin's man and Odin demands a sacrifice. That is the old way. If you argue, you will only bring his anger on your head too.' His eyes were iron as he stared at Egil. 'I am ready to die.'

'But are you not afraid?' Egil asked, his tone almost pleading. 'The blood eagle, it is such a terrible death.'

'My Lord suffered a terrible death,' the monk stated calmly. 'Crucified on a cross. But He rose again. Tomorrow, if it be His will, I shall take my place beside Him in Paradise.' He shook his head gravely. 'Why should I fear death when I am promised life eternal?'

'Then you want to die?' Egil pressed incredulously.

The monk shrugged, but the first time Egil saw his boldness waver. 'I am resigned to it,' he replied quietly, 'for it seems it must be.'

Egil glanced across at his sleeping companions. His

eyes caught the Thor's hammer that hung from Sigurd's wrist. It struck him in an instant that in shape it was not so very different from the cross the monk wore round his neck. There were jewellers back home, he knew, whose moulds could make either symbol: the hammer or the cross. Vikings, Christians, they were no longer so far apart – though Sigurd and those like him would never admit or allow it. The world was moving on.

He turned back to the monk. 'Tell me more about yourself,' he said, 'about your land, your people, your faith. I wish to learn.'

As the storm prowled outside, occasionally howling along the tunnel, the two young men talked, seemingly oblivious to the precariousness of the situation. They spoke easily, as if friends of many years' standing.

At last, the torch began to gutter. Then Egil picked up his knife, walked over to his captive and quickly cut through the ropes that bound him.

'Are you sure, Egil Egilsson?' the monk whispered. 'Cutting these ropes, you cut your own ties too. There is no returning.'

Egil nodded. What did he have to return to anyway, he thought? Erik Blood-Axe's reign in York could not last. He had already been overthrown once and might be again at any moment. There was no one left back in his own country that he loved. Certainly he had no wish any more to follow his brutal cousin. It was time for a new beginning, for new inspiration.

'We can go east,' the monk said, rubbing his chafed wrists. 'There is a community of monks there who will make us welcome. For some time I had planned to go there.'

Egil nodded purposefully. Then he turned and, reaching down, picked up the jewelled chalice. 'Here, take this,' he said to his new friend.

But the monk shook his head. 'No, leave it,' he commanded. 'Who needs such worthless treasures? We have much greater things to worry about.'

Egil looked at him questioningly.

'Souls, Egil Egilsson, souls,' the monk smiled. 'Come!'

Hitching his robe a little and stooping, he stepped forward into the dark tunnel.

After a last glance around the gloomy hive-like chamber, taking in the bone-strewn floor upon which his fellow Norseman slept still, Egil Egilsson too departed. He went after the monk along the tunnel and through the narrow gap, once filled by the large stone.

Outside the storm slumbered in the wind's soft keening. The golden wings of dawn glimmered on the dark horizon.

Following his companion, Egil moved towards the light.

11th
CENTURY

————★————

THERESA BRESLIN

A FALCON FOR A QUEEN

Illustrated by Sarah Young

THERESA BRESLIN

A FALCON FOR A QUEEN

It was an easy jump. From the spur of the rock overlooking the approach of the castle keep at Dunfermline, to the top of the wooden palisade at the sentry outpost. He'd done it many times. An easy jump, and the perfect place for a boy of his age who liked to watch the King and his soldiers galloping past.

But today Euan slipped. His foot turned beneath him and he fell, right into the path of the mounted outriders.

There was a shout. The lead horse stumbled, the rider

missed his stirrup and was down.

Euan was first to his feet, and offered his arm to aid the man. The knight thrust him aside.

'Cur's whelp,' he snarled, and raising his gloved fist he struck Euan across the face.

The boy gasped and fell to his knees, tasting blood in his mouth.

'What's amiss here, Earl Rolf?'

King Malcolm himself had ridden to the front of the royal procession.

'Some trickery,' cried the English knight. He looked around wildly. 'Ambush and kidnap!'

'There is no treachery here.' The King laughed loudly. 'This is Euan, the Falconer's boy. We see him often enough, perched like one of his own birds on that gatepost.' Malcolm leant from his saddle and pulled Euan to his feet. 'The boy will be curious to know why we have so many royal visitors today.' He waved his hand at the line of richly-dressed people behind him. 'The arrival of noble Edgar, Saxon prince and heir to the throne of England, with his mother and sisters, has made quite a stir within the town.'

''Twas fate that wrecked our ships and drove us to landfall here.' Earl Rolf glared around him, at the wild

Scottish hills with the bleak North Sea in the distance. Then he muttered under his breath, 'We would not by choice land in such a barbaric place.'

'Fate indeed,' said King Malcolm. And then added under his own breath, 'But it was also William, the conqueror from Normandy, who snatched your kingdom and forced you to flee.'

'The boy requires aid.' A lady's voice interrupted the two men.

Malcolm swivelled in his saddle to see who had spoken.

Margaret, elder of the two English princesses, had spurred her garron forward. Her pretty face showed concern. 'See! His lip is bleeding,' she said.

'So, he bleeds.' The King spoke abruptly. 'It will teach the young pup to be more agile.'

'The boy is hurt,' the lady persisted. 'Let me help.'

Euan quickly wiped his sleeve across his face. ''Tis nothing,' he said.

'No!' Margaret cried out. And to everyone's astonishment she dismounted and stood in front of Euan.

'What is your name?' she asked.

Euan kept his head down. 'Euan,' he mumbled.

Margaret tilted up his head with her fingers. Then

she took an embroidered cloth from her sleeve and staunched the flow of blood. 'There, Euan,' she smiled at him. 'Now, would you hold my stirrup while I remount?'

Once back in the saddle she turned to King Malcolm. 'Forgive me,' she said. 'I could not in conscience leave the boy, wounded as he was by one of my own knights.'

An unquiet silence fell among the mounted men. Their King was known for his rages and rough ways. How would he now speak to this young woman who had openly defied him?

The English princess smiled at King Malcolm. 'I am sorry to have delayed our progress when you have offered us such kind hospitality in our time of trouble.'

Malcolm looked for a long moment at Margaret. 'Welcome you are,' he said finally.

Euan stood aside and watched the royal procession once more begin to move forward. As it passed, he raised his fingers to touch his swollen mouth. And then Euan looked down. Still grasped in his hand was the square of cloth on which was daintily embroidered the letter M.

Euan was kept busy in the mews, and it was several days before he saw the princess Margaret again. He knew that she walked out each day beyond the castle gate to devotions at the little chapel of the Columban monks. It seemed that she spent many hours praying, and that her sweet ways changed all who came in contact with her. All that is, save the King.

'A great King for Scotland,' Euan's father said one morning as he and Euan fed the birds. 'For Scotland was not, before Malcolm was.' He stroked the peregrine falcon. 'But ill manners are not seemly in royalty, or indeed in any man.' He grinned at Euan as they saw Margaret's slight figure crossing the courtyard. 'Though there is one whose gentle ways could bring to heel the fiercest hound.'

Euan took the dainty cloth from inside his tunic and ran to catch her up. 'Lady, you have been walking out?' he said as he returned it to her.

'Scotland is very beautiful,' replied Margaret. 'There is much to see.'

'But you should not wander far. It is not safe,' said Euan.

'I have no fear. King Malcolm keeps his kingdom well,' she said. 'They tell me that by his royal grace the countryside is safe to travel.'

'His word is law,' Euan agreed. 'The King's rule is

kept.' I wonder if they also tell you that it is because his punishments are harsh, he thought to himself.

They had by now reached the castle door. Euan began to take his leave of her, when suddenly she said, 'May I come and see you with your birds some day?'

And so it became her habit to come often to the mews and watch Euan and his father with the falcons. Euan was working with a young merlin hawk, trying to train the bird to sit upon the leather gauntlet which he wore. He held a piece of meat firmly in his fingers, coaxing her to step from her wooden stoop on to his gloved arm. All the time he spoke quietly to her. Before many days had passed, he had but to raise his arm and she would come and sit upon his wrist.

'Such wild creatures,' Margaret said in wonder, 'and yet they obey you. Your strictures must be firm.'

'Gentled, never forced,' said Euan, not noticing that the King himself had approached behind him.

'Yes,' Margaret agreed. 'Living things respond to kindness,' she said, 'not violence.' She touched the bruise still coloured on Euan's cheek. Then she met the King's eyes and did not look away.

One day, past noon, Euan heard someone shouting his

name. King Malcolm was hurrying towards him, calling as he came. 'See you, now, boy. The lady Margaret, has she been this way today?'

'No, Sire,' said Euan. He looked in bewilderment at the trail of people following the King: Margaret's mother, sister, and brother. 'Is she lost?'

'Aye,' grunted Malcolm, 'from daybreak. She set out for morning prayers but has not since been seen.' His face was set and lined. 'You could not guess where she might be?'

'She halts many times on her way to give alms to any poor on the road,' said Euan.

'I know it,' snapped the King. 'And strangely, there are often many poor whatever road she takes.' He smiled then, and added, 'Such a kindly lady.'

'She visits a sick child in a forester's cott,' said Margaret's mother. 'Perhaps she went there, and missed the way.'

Euan and Malcolm looked at each other. They both knew that there were wolves in the forest.

'Find your father,' said Malcolm quickly. 'Get the dogs. I'll rouse the garrison.'

They were ready and mounted in less than ten minutes. On a sudden impulse Euan pulled on his buckskin hawking gauntlet, and called the merlin to him.

Margaret had indeed been to see the forester's child, but where she had gone after, the woman did not know.

'She is not in castle, town, nor road,' said the sergeant-at-arms. 'It must be the forest.'

Once in the forest Euan held his fist high, and turning into the wind, he cast off the merlin. The bird flew to a tree, and perched, watching. Euan called her back and she came at once and settled on his wrist. He spoke softly as they rode on.

'Ho, my bonny bird. Messenger of the sky. Can you see aught?'

The merlin put her head to the side and blinked an amber eye.

'Lord of the air. Farrand falcon. Use your eyes. For me.' Euan's voice lilted.

King Malcolm turned his head and looked at Euan. His brow furrowed but he said nothing.

Euan whispered again to the bird, and then he raised his arm and the merlin flew. Wings beating, gaining height, she soared, stooped, then soared again.

They went deeper and deeper into the great wood.

Each turning circle of the bird's became wider and higher as the afternoon wore on, and each time she took longer to return. Euan kept her fed with titbits from his falconer's bag.

Then towards evening, the merlin did not come back.

They had paused beside a river to give the horses time to drink. Euan studied the sky anxiously.

'The bird will have gone home,' said his father.

'As we should,' one of the men said, taking care to keep his voice low. 'This is a lost cause.'

'The King knows it,' said Euan's father. 'But a man in love will not give up so easily.'

In love! Euan stared at his father. Malcolm in love with Margaret! He had not thought of this. But now that his father had spoken the words, it was plain to see. The way Malcolm looked at the young princess, how he spoke to her, sought out her company.

And what did she think, Euan wondered? But then, suddenly, he knew what she thought. Of course she cared for Malcolm, he realised with a jolt. A day did not pass that she did not speak of the King.

'By your leave, Sire. Perhaps we should wait now until sunrise?'

The King looked at his sergeant-at-arms. 'No,' he

said. 'If she is lying injured, then come daybreak she will have perished with the cold. We will return to the castle, change horses and men, and with lighted brands we will go on looking through the night.'

As they clattered into the courtyard, Margaret's mother and sister ran forward.

'Nothing,' the King said dully.

The horses were changed, and the torches lit. Euan checked the mews.

The merlin was not home.

Fresh soldiers and horses were ready. The King swung himself into his saddle. 'Are you coming, boy?' he asked Euan.

Euan nodded. Behind the King's head the trees of the forest threw shadows in the sky, the far Lomond hills were blue in the distance... and something else.

Euan screwed up his eyes. A bird was winging home, its silhouette on the evening sky. It was the merlin.

Set against the sinking sun, Euan could not at first see that she held something in her talons. The merlin swept past him and landed on her wooden stoop. She fluttered and preened, and then dropped the muddied object.

Euan ran forward to pick it up. It was a square of

cloth, earth-stained and soiled, embroidered on one side with the letter M.

They found her within the hour. She had tripped on a tree root and her ankle had turned beneath her.

'As yours did, Euan, that first day we met,' she smiled across at him from where she was now sitting at the front of King Malcolm's saddle. She looked up at the King. 'I thank you, Sire, for finding me.'

'Not me to thank,' Malcolm replied gruffly. ''Twas the boy, Euan, and his gentled hawk.' He looked down at her and spoke slowly. 'Lady, I acknowledge that your wisdom holds true. Kind regard does indeed beget loyalty and love.'

Some months later Malcolm and Margaret were married at Dunfermline Priory. As the bridal procession wound its way from the castle to the church, Euan rode beside the lady Margaret. On his arm he carried the merlin. A falcon for a Queen.

12th
CENTURY

———— ✦ ————

BERNARD ASHLEY

THE MASK

Illustrated by David Wyatt

BERNARD ASHLEY

THE MASK

The boys of Pubungu village were sick with tiredness
and they hurt with the tribal cuts on their cheeks.
Tomorrow they would be men, tomorrow would be the
climax – the dance they would do for the chief,
Isingoma, who was visiting their village to claim cattle.

Kantu was as tired as the rest of the boys, but still he
had to finish the mask he would wear in the dance. The
injury he'd done to his hand in the mock fighting was
making it hard for him. A sharpened stave had glanced

off his shield and pierced him in the soft flesh between his thumb and his first finger. Now, sitting in the doorway, he had to work on by the light of the cold second stone in the sky while the other boys were already snoring or sleep-mumbling in the round hut.

He scraped with the blade of his knife and he dug with its point. He made slits for the eyes and holes for the sharp nose. There was dyed black raffia for the hair, and a line of pierced holes all round the jaw for tying the mask to his own face with thongs. But with his injured hand it was difficult work.

The hut had been the boys' home since the rains. Under Bala the elder they had learned how to herd the cattle, frighten lions and make shelter and fire. At the end, under the spirit of Ruhanga the creator of the earth and the sky, their faces had been cut for manhood in the tribal pattern, then rubbed with sacred ashes from the wood of the Omuko tree. Tomorrow the ten of them would drive out bad spirits in the traditional *mbuya* dance, but this year not just for the village but for the tribal chief.

Kantu's hand bled, with the injury and with the stabs he had given himself making the mask. His face hurt and itched and he kept stopping to rub it. At last, though, he had finished. He tied his mask to the roof sticks and lay himself on the fronded floor to sleep. All too soon the first stone would be in the sky again.

They were a brave sight, these new men in their dance circle. The girls and the younger boys drew back from their tasselled ankles. Who each one was, whose brother, whose uncle, was a mystery; the *mbuya* masks they wore on their faces disguised them all.

Kantu could see out, though. Through the eye slits and the nostril holes he could see a blur of faces and feet. He could see his family standing with the rest, rigid because Chief Isingoma was here today, and the chief was fierce. A wave to the earth of his swat would have a villager dragged away to be speared. But Kantu could not see Bikira, the girl he would take for his wife one day – and he soon saw why.

When Chief Isingoma came into the kraal, Bikira was walking behind him, with a necklet of beads around her neck. Bikira was his property! From all the girls in the village the chief had chosen her to help tend his herd of white cows. And by tradition, that night Isingoma would take her to the holy Omuko tree to give a sacrifice to make her bear his children. Then as well as by day she would have to tend him by night. Bikira! Not to be Kantu's wife any more but to be a wife of Isingoma! She was too young, and Isingoma was old. When he died she would have to lie down and be buried with him...

But on the blast of a horn Kantu was pushed into the dance. The *mbuya* beat started drumming, and with voices driving the evil spirits away, Kantu and the new men stamped and wailed in their circle. Immediately, Chief Isingoma separated himself from Bikira and jumped into the middle. His hard eyes stared at each dancer as he pointed a bony finger, working round the dance. But at Kantu's turn Isingoma suddenly threw back his head and shouted and waved his swat in a frantic way.

'The eyes!' he shouted at Kantu's masked face. '*Big* eyes! This Pubungu has big *Kimera* eyes!'

Kimera was Isingoma's younger brother, who had fought a war with him to settle who should be the chief. Now Kimera lived in further lands with his own smaller tribe, a deadly enemy, always waiting to pounce.

The drumming throbbed on, the dancing pounded on, and this was what saved Kantu – some thought the chief was joining in the dance as he high-stamped in anger. But Kantu knew. The hard old eyes and the fierce finger stayed pointing at him; Isingoma saw bad magic in the way Kantu's mask was the Kimera shape, all the fault of his injured hand. In a short blink the swat would be raised to the sky, then thrust down to the earth with a cry of 'Death!' and Isingoma's bodyguard would drag Kantu from the circle.

Like a spear of lightning himself Kantu suddenly turned and leapt over the youngers, ran round the elders, and sped on his fastest chase-jackal feet for the open. None of the villagers barred him, for he could have been any of their sons; but when he was out of the kraal he snatched off his mask so he could see, threw it into a thorn bush, and ran for his life.

Zig-zagging through scrub the way he'd been taught, he kept below the earth rim not to be seen. He broke no branches, and he ran where the short grass grew so he wouldn't leave his track – until at last he could run no longer, and he had to wait for his loud panting to be stilled so that he could listen.

But they had given up – or had never started, knowing they would catch him stealing milk or grabbing grain sometime; everyone had to keep alive.

Meanwhile he rested, and when he had rested he walked on, following the direction of the bright stone in the sky which was turning red.

His heart was under the darkest cloud. He was not a Pubungu any more. Through his bad mask-making he could never return to his village, he was an outcast from the tribe. He had no Pubungu brothers, neither men nor boys, and he had lost his promised wife to Isingoma. Alone in the bush he could be wounded by jackal or eaten by lion. With a partner, one can watch while the other sleeps; but a man on his own could soon be an offering for the circling birds of death, his bones carried days apart from each other by hungry, running beasts. But the pain of the elder's knife, the no-sleep of the night before and the hard running from the village had drained him of all energy. He made a swift search for shelter upwind of the jungle thicket where lion and jackal lived, and within twenty breaths of putting his head on to his crooked arm he was asleep…

'Pubungu!'

… to be awakened by the cruellest voice, to see the fiercest sight – the masked face of a spirit man, and judging by the wide eyes of the mask, a Kimera warrior.

'You spy? You watchdog? You traitor from Isingoma?'

'No! No!'

'Come!'

He was pulled roughly to his feet by others, pinched and pushed and beaten round the head and forced to go with them to where spotted cattle grazed. In the kraal beyond, beaten out of breath and bruised with the pinching, he was flung into a tall, hide-covered hut, before a man sitting on a mound of skins.

Kimera, the brother of Isingoma, in the gloom.

'Why you here?' Kimera demanded. In his hand he held not a swat but a zebra tail. He held it loosely, hanging down, but Kantu knew it would soon be used to give the same death message…

'I want brothers. I want tribe,' Kantu pleaded. 'Isingoma thinks me bad, but I am good. I am – ' he tried to stand up tall – 'I am man.'

Kimera rose and came towards him. Up close he was younger than Isingoma, and his eyes were not so hard. He pointed a finger at Kantu's cheek, cut and ashened.

'Not Kimera,' he said. His fingers rubbed roughly in the sore scars which were Kantu's tribal marks. 'Cut can never change. Never Kimera.' He raised the zebra tail from his side to his shoulder, then into the air. Now it would come down to point at the earth and Kantu would be killed.

'I know where Isingoma will be in the cold light,' Kantu suddenly said. 'Where he will be alone with a new wife.'

The zebra tail remained in the air, then it was lowered slowly.

'Where this?'

'The holy Omuko Tree.'

Chief Kimera snorted. 'Many holy Omuko trees! Ruhanga make one for each tribe, to hold up its sky. Where *this* tree?'

'I show you.'

Kimera thought about it, but in the way of a strong chief, without looking at his attendants. Suddenly he clicked his fingers, sharply and loud. 'You show!' he said.

They went, Kimera and Kantu and none other, for the fight of brother with brother to be the chief is for brothers alone. Chiefs rule through pride. Wars are different – then all the warriors do battle. But for a chief alone at a holy tree, there would be a fight but no war. It would be single blood combat.

Kantu knew what he was risking, going there, and so did Kimera. Isingoma's holy Omuko tree was in his own tribal territory, in the lands of the white cattle, where Isingoma guards would prowl. But custom said he should go alone with his new wife to the tree, where no-one would hear him asking blessing. Chiefs needed blessings, but it was shaming to hear them beseeching Ruhanga.

Kantu led the way. He knew that if he tried any trick he would surely be as doomed as the white calf which Isingoma would take to the tree. Kimera was a strong and clever warrior – he would despatch Kantu with one fierce thrust of his spear.

They went along the sedgeland of the long water where tracks and scents disappeared. They took the steep climb up the overhang from which poorly-formed babies were thrown. No-one came to the holy tree this way; Isingoma would have walked with his new wife along the path of the chief. That path would be guarded, the steep climb would not.

When they came to it, the tree shone white in the light of the second stone. It was so tall that its top could not be seen by night for it was holding up the sky, while its lower trunk was twisted into long arm-like roots above the ground, reaching out to those who came for blessing. In one of the grooves between the roots Isingoma would sleep, with Bikira in another. The next night she would be taken to lie in his chief's hut.

As Kantu and Kimera approached, the sound of

Isingoma's voice could be heard. He was calling to Ruhanga to make holy the blood of the dead calf which he would smear on Bikira's belly, to bless her with the fatness of children. The same blood he would rub upon himself. The sound of these words, the thought of Bikira and the old chief lying together overwhelmed Kantu with anger, and with sudden strength. He was an outcast. He would rush forward and kill the chief by his own hand.

But Kimera must have seen inside his head, into his thoughts, as if Kantu's face were itself a mask which could be taken off to reveal the spirit.

'No!' he said, in a low voice. 'Kimera!' – although it was then shouted. '*Kimera*!' And he ran forward to the Omuko tree where Isingoma was lying prone.

At the sound of the shout Isingoma came to his feet, but only because Kimera let him. Brother did not fight brother like cowards. Kimera raised his spear, but gave Isingoma time to grab his own and raise it.

'I claim Isingoma tribe,' Kimera said. 'You, old and stupid. Me, young and strong.' The brothers, both sons of the first chief Kyomya, faced each other. There would be a fight. One would win and rule the lands of both the white and the spotted cattle. The other would be dead.

But suddenly, from another groove in the tree's roots, ran Bikira.

'Kantu!' She ran to him. And now it struck Kantu. If Kimera won, as new chief *he* could claim her; she was young and beautiful. If Isingoma won, he would keep her. Whoever won, Bikira would be claimed as a wife and he would be put to death.

'Come!' he shouted to Bikira, and pulled her away towards the steep descent where there were no guards, running fast, Bikira throwing off Isingoma's necklace. Kantu knew that neither of the chiefs could move to stop him – one step away, one look away – and the other would throw the first spear. The brothers were to fight, and there would be much of the second stone in the sky before Kantu and Bikira could be followed.

If they were followed. If Kimera won, perhaps he would be grateful for being shown the secret Omuko tree where Isingoma was alone. If Isingoma won, perhaps he would be busy claiming Kimera's herds.

So they ran and ran together, through the pain of running themselves exhausted, and on further still to far plains. Tomorrow the new man and his chosen wife would start travelling many bright stones away, watching for each other. And with skills and hard work they might find cattle of their own, and begin a new tribe, where the masks had eyes as wide as Kantu chose to make them.

13th CENTURY

———✦———

JENNY NIMMO

THE DEATH OF A PRINCE

Illustrated by Mark Robertson

JENNY NIMMO

THE DEATH OF A PRINCE

He was born with a crooked foot and named Dylan, after an uncle who had vanished into the sea. Later it was discovered that the boy's eyesight was none too good either, so he would be useless with a longbow. A sword would be out of the question, he was so puny. His family needed soldiers.

His father, Iorwerth ap Owain, was a great soldier and one of Prince Llywelyn's favourites. He held land to the west of Snowdonia, the great wall of mountains that made Gwynedd safest of all the Welsh kingdoms. Not that the men of Gwynedd weren't always on their guard. The English King, Edward, was a ruthless and hungry ruler, and Llywelyn was a thorn in his side. Brilliant and brave, Llywelyn had been acknowledged by the other Welsh princes as their overlord – Prince of all the Welsh. Even Edward's father, Henry, had recognised Llywelyn's independence, allowing him to rule Wales as he wanted.

But now Henry was dead. Edward was very different from his father. He was determined to conquer Wales. Llywelyn was equally determined that it should be free.

Dylan was three years old when he first heard the name of Edward. His older brothers, Rhys, Owain and Madog, were discussing the new English King when a great trembling overcame Dylan. Words clattered in his head but he was too afraid to speak them: 'Edward the wolf. Edward assassin. Edward, the end.' In his mind he saw a tall man, young and strong, his black hair curling and abundant, his legs very long. He had a lean and hungry look. This was Dylan's first vision.

As Dylan's trembling increased his mother sat him by the fire and his sister, Gwenllian, tried to soothe him with her harp, but his father said, 'That child is lacking in sense. He's useless.'

Rhys and Owain began to laugh, but Madog said, 'Don't mock him. Dylan is right to tremble. Who knows what the future holds?'

Ten years went by. Dylan at thirteen was small for his age, quiet and always dreaming. He turned his dreaming into poetry and, carrying his words in his head, he would go into the mountains and match them to the sound of the cold streams, the wind and the calls of the ever-present melancholy buzzards. Sometimes his words would sing over the rocks, up to the peak of Snowdon, the highest mountain of all. But when he came back to the house, his poetry would wither, stifled by the noise of dogs, his brothers' warlike shouting and the brooding atmosphere of battle.

In the year 1282, King Edward's troops marched into Wales and surrounded Snowdonia. Wales held its breath until winter, when a blinding snowstorm drove off the English. Not to be outdone, Edward sent a force round to the north, to attack Llywelyn's soldiers where they might be more vulnerable. The English force was destroyed. Prince Llywelyn was safe – if he stayed where he was.

One morning Dylan woke up with a feeling of dread. Late the previous night his brothers had returned from a skirmish on the borders of Powys. All three were experienced soldiers now. They were bruised and weary but, thank God, not badly wounded. Dylan tried to hide his fear that morning, but the shudder that travelled up his spine shook his fingers as though it would have him play some ghostly instrument. He spilled a bowl of steaming broth on Owain's bare foot and Owain screamed, 'You fool! You useless idiot! I've survived a battle only to be ruined by my own brother.'

'I'm sorry, Owain. Sorry, sorry! Please forgive!' Dylan hung his head.

Madog, always the kindest, caught hold of Dylan's hands and, looking hard into his eyes, asked, 'What is it, little brother? What do you see?'

'Magpies,' Dylan murmured. 'Magpies in a column on the ground, and they are humming.'

'Magpies don't hum,' scoffed Rhys. 'Magpies screech like ill-fitting doors.'

'They are saying their prayers,' mumbled Dylan. A strange image threatened to break through the column of birds but Dylan closed his mind against it.

Gwenllian ran up with a bowl of water to bathe Owain's scalded foot, and Dylan lurched away from Madog murmuring, 'Sorry. Sorry.' His lame foot caught on a stool and he tumbled to the floor. He was glad his father wasn't there to see his foolishness.

Iorwerth ap Owain came late that night with a small troop of soldiers. The faithful greyhounds set up a frenzied barking long before their master reached the house, and wouldn't stop their noise until he had petted every one of them. Twenty or so men crowded into the house for a meal. Later some would have to sleep in the stables, the floor space not being adequate to accommodate them all. The weary soldiers sprawled before the fire, comforted by Gwenllian's spiritual music. They began to murmur among themselves and Dylan, crouching in the dark, listened to the news of war.

Prince Llywelyn had left his stronghold and was travelling south to put new heart into his allies, the princes of Gower and Deheubarth. 'And from there he will go into the valley of the Wye, to talk to the Marcher barons,' someone stated.

'A risky enterprise,' said one of the older soldiers. 'Those barons on the border are neither for the Welsh nor the English. They think only of themselves. They will sway in the wind, first with Wales, then with England.'

'True. They do not keep their word,' said another.

13

In the crush of warm bodies, Dylan shivered. He stood up and, gazing at the firelight, he began to speak.

The soldiers turned from the fire and listened.

Dylan knew that his words were beautiful, but they were not what his father wanted to hear, for they formed themselves into a lament, a dirge and a terrible prayer.

'Our guests don't need these dark words,' his father muttered.

No. Dylan knew they would rather have a hopeful and heroic poem, words to give them courage and inspiration.

'Pay him no heed. My son's a fool,' said Iorwerth.

But the soldiers listened. They couldn't help themselves. When Dylan reached the conclusion of his lament, unknown names – Cilmeri, Irfon and Cwm Hir – fell from his lips, and then the thing that had lain hidden behind the column of magpies revealed itself to him: a headless body. And Dylan told what he saw in words as sharp and beautiful as diamonds.

'Cwm Hir,' he said again, 'the long valley.'

'Enough!' His father towered over him. 'Leave us!'

Now that the words were out of him, Dylan felt empty and ashamed. He shuffled through the crowd of bemused soldiers and out into the dark. The door closed behind him with a magpie screech.

'I think I am banished,' he murmured. He heard Madog's voice calling him home, but he stumbled on. Leaving the road, he struck out blindly towards the mountains. And still Madog's voice pursued him.

'Dylan! Dylan, come back!'

He couldn't go back. He had insulted his father's guests. He had filled them with despair instead of hope. Tonight they would lie sleepless and troubled and, at dawn, they would rise without having rested, their hearts heavy with dread.

I have shamed my father, he thought. He brought his men to our house for warmth and comfort, for songs of heroism. But I couldn't help telling what I saw. Perhaps it is all rubbish. How will I ever know?

He walked on, through the cold night – now upon a sheep track, now stumbling over frozen streams and boulders. His feet were bare and he had nothing but a thin cloak over his linen tunic. He couldn't tell if his shivering came from fear or the cold.

At length he came to a tiny dwelling set into the mountainside. He could smell peat smoke and knew a fire burned inside. Dylan knocked and the door was opened by an old man. His face softened when he saw it was only a boy who had woken him. Behind him, his wife muttered, 'Pity the child.' She drew Dylan inside, sat him by the fire and bathed his frozen feet. Then she set a bowl of broth before him.

He smiled his gratitude, but when he attempted to thank them, he found he couldn't make a sound. He rubbed his throat, opening his mouth as wide as he could, but it was useless.

'Poor boy,' said the old man. 'He's worse than the sheep, he cannot even bleat.'

Dylan stayed with the old couple through December, helping with the animals, carrying water from the stream and chopping firewood as best he could. They treated him like one of the many sons they'd lost: some dead in battle, others too frail to survive the harsh mountain weather. The old folk seemed to live in a world of their own. No news reached them, no hint of the dreadful events that were occurring throughout the Welsh kingdoms.

One day in early January, a snowstorm blew up. Icy flakes swept down from the summit of Snowdon, and the old couple hurried their small flock under cover.

Soon the snow had buried everything in sight. Dylan was in the wood below the house, gathering dry twigs for the fire. As he watched the snow's steady fall, a strange quiet descended on the mountain. The wind's howl died and the sighing trees fell silent.

Dylan looked at the thick wall of snow that lay between him and the house and realised that he was trapped in the freezing wood. A night spent in the snow would be the end even of the strongest man. Already Dylan was beginning to feel the icy hand of death at his back. Even if he had been able to call out to the old couple, they couldn't have reached him. So he drew his ragged cloak around him and prepared to spend the night huddled against the trunk of a broad oak. Fate would decide if he lived or died.

In the eerie silence that surrounded him, time ceased to exist, so when the moon appeared, he didn't know how long he had been sitting in the dark. The wood was suddenly transformed into a place of startling beauty. The snow that filtered through the branches shone like crystals, and every snow-clad tree was turned to marble.

In the distance, moving through the avenue of shining tree pillars, he glimpsed a snow-white horse. As the animal drew closer its rider became visible, and

Dylan could see that on his silvery hair, the man wore a slim gold crown. The horse approached Dylan at a gentle pace, his footfalls on the icy ground quite soundless.

When horse and rider drew abreast of the motionless boy, they stopped and the man looked down. He smiled at Dylan, a tender embracing smile, and then he unpinned his cloak and threw it to the boy. It settled over Dylan, soft and warm as a blanket of feathers. He tried to murmur his thanks but suddenly the horse reared up and galloped away. In a moment the stranger and his mount had been swallowed by the snow.

The cloak that covered Dylan drew him into a deep sleep, and when he woke he felt as warm as though he had spent the night beside a fire.

The dawn sky streamed with colour and when the sun burst over the mountains the snowfield beyond the wood was already beginning to thaw. Now the snow was only knee-deep and Dylan managed to wade right up to the house. When he pushed open the door, the two old folk leapt from their rush-bed with screams of terror. They thought he had surely perished in the night and now his ghost stood on the threshold.

When they realised that Dylan was flesh and blood

they hugged and fussed over him, muttering about miracles and magic, but Dylan, finding a voice at last, told them, 'It was the stranger's cloak.'

They stared at Dylan, speechless with astonishment.

'You spoke, my son!' cried the old woman, hugging him all the harder, but the old man said, 'What stranger? No one can have passed by on such a fierce night.'

Dylan lifted the cloak from his shoulders. It was only a plain woollen thing, but it had saved his life.

'Who?' the old folk demanded. 'Who gave you this cloak?'

'Heaven's white land now is his home,' Dylan murmured. His head was full of words again. He didn't know their source, but his old friends clasped each other's hands, enthralled by the young boy's voice.

His poetry rang out through the thick walls and climbed to the sky where it could scarcely be distinguished from the voices of the lonely buzzards. But Madog ap Iorwerth, riding his mare through the wood, heard the melancholy lilting voice and knew he had found his brother.

Leaving his mare in the wood, Madog walked on foot up to the snow-covered dwelling. All winter he had been searching for Dylan but somehow he had never found this small farm beyond the oak wood. His family had told him to give up the search – his little brother must be dead, they said. But Madog would not give up.

'My heart tells me that Dylan is alive,' he told them, 'and I care too much for him to let him vanish from my life. He is a poet and a prophet and I will not rest until I find him.'

Now, hearing that golden voice gliding through the air, he began to bound towards it over the steep field of snow. Flinging wide the door of the little house, Madog gazed into a dark room that seemed to be full of animals: goats, sheep, dogs and even a pig. The old couple had brought in all the animals that could not be housed in the flimsy stable. In the centre of this menagerie stood Dylan.

The two brothers fell into each other's arms. When the old people had recovered from their astonishment, they welcomed their visitor with traditional hospitality, washing Madog's weary feet and offering every last morsel from their larder.

'I'm sorry we don't have a harp to entertain you,' said the old woman wistfully.

'You have my brother,' said Madog, 'and his magic

words. But now he must come home with me.'

Dylan shook his head. 'I can't come home. I'm useless. I disgraced my father's house with my thoughtless words.'

'Not thoughtless, Dylan. You saw the future.'

Madog's grave tone made Dylan's heart miss a beat. 'How's that?' he asked.

'You told us of... of an event,' said Madog, 'at Cilmeri near the river Irfon. And you spoke of a headless body in the Long Valley.'

Dylan whispered, 'Yes?'

'Our great Llywelyn, Prince of all the Welsh, was killed at Cilmeri. Madog's eyes glistened. 'His head was struck off and carried round Wales by the victorious English. Now it is being mocked in London. The heart has gone out of us, little brother. We are a defeated nation.'

The old couple fell to their knees, weeping and praying.

Now, when Dylan most needed words, he could utter none. At last he murmured, 'But the magpies? Why were the magpies praying?'

'Not magpies, Dylan. I believe that you saw monks. A procession of Cistercian monks in their black and white robes could easily be mistaken for magpies. You saw them at a distance, a distance of days. The monks took the body of our prince to the Abbey Cwm Hir, and buried it there.'

'The heart has not gone out of Wales,' Dylan said quietly.

This seemed to comfort Madog. 'I must take you back to our family,' he said. 'After these sad events they don't doubt that you're a prophet and a poet, just as I was always trying to tell them. Our family longs for your return.'

'No,' said Dylan.

'We treasure you, Dylan,' Madog insisted. 'If soldiers can be felled then we must turn to poets. Your words are precious, they keep our language safe.'

His brother spoke so sincerely, Dylan had no choice but to believe him. Though foretelling a tragedy seemed a hard way to become accepted as a poet. He bid the old folk farewell, promising to visit them again within the month.

'I'll bring you a horse,' Madog told them, 'for you must surely need one. And I'll bring flour and corn, enough to last till summer.'

The old woman clung to Dylan. 'Once again we're

losing a son,' she moaned.

'Oh no! Not at all,' said Madog. 'I and my brothers are all your sons now. Our family will be forever in your debt.'

With some reluctance the old woman let Dylan go, and the two brothers walked down to the wood where Madog had tethered his mare. He helped Dylan on to her back and climbed up behind him. But before his brother turned the mare towards the trees, Dylan said, 'I spent the night in this wood,' and he told Madog about the stranger on the white horse, and his mysterious woollen cloak.

Madog was silent for a moment, and then he asked, 'Do you believe it was our lost prince whom you saw?'

'I know it,' Dylan said. 'And I know that he was on his way to Snowdon's summit. I don't see him as a headless prince, lying in a dark valley. I see him standing on the white roof of the world, gazing on his country.'

Madog looked up at the snowclouds that presently hid the highest peak. It seemed to him that beyond the clouds the sun was shining. The prince on the summit would be bathed in gold.

Observing his brother's uplifted face, Dylan said,

'I've made you smile, Madog.'

'That's what poets are for,' said Madog.

14th
CENTURY

———— ★ ————

GERALDINE MCCAUGHREAN

'WHY WOULD I LIE?'

Illustrated by Sarah Young

Geraldine McCaughrean

'Why Would I Lie?'

Look at my hands. The rheumatism is so bad; they look as if I'm holding two fistfuls of stones. I dropped the quill just now and it took me ten minutes to pick it up again. I'd give the whole world for a new pair of hands. The whole world.

He was lucky. He went to his grave all but perfect. And so quick: like stepping through a door into another world. I cried like a baby the day my master died. To think I meant from the very start to murder him.

We set off from England on St Michael's Day 1322, on pilgrimage to the Holy Places – Sir John Mandeville and his manservant Clym. Sir John was a learned man and a great writer-down of his thoughts. Nightly he wrote in his diary – except after a drop too much wine, when I wrote it up for him. He taught me to write, so I was able. That was useful: I knew I ought to be able to read and write if I was going to pass myself off as a gentleman.

During dinner Sir John would prop up a book before him and read out to me what other travellers had written about the next place on our route – Cyprus or Constantinople or Jerusalem. It was dull stuff, the way they wrote it. When we came to the places ourselves – pushing through the crowds, tripping over the beggars – Sir John would say, 'They didn't mention the colour! They never said about the smell!'

We visited a *lot* of holy relics. Some days it seemed to me as if saints must explode at the point of death, and teeth and ribs and head and hands and blood scatter across Christendom for people to keep in silver caskets and venerate. A strange look came over Sir John whenever he visited holy relics. He seemed to be trying to see right through the gold and jewels to the thing inside – some anklebone or splinter of wood from Noah's Ark. 'Astounding, isn't it,' I said once, 'that a piece of old hair can work miracles?'

'The question is, Clym…' said he, wearing that peculiar look of his, '… is it TRUE?'

I was taken aback. 'Well, churches wouldn't *lie*, would they?'

'Hmmm,' was all he said. He was a great stickler for the truth, Sir John. The times I heard him say, 'Yes Clym, but is it TRUE?'

While he talked to monks and scholars about local history and politics, I preferred the company of sailors and travelling merchants. They told me the interesting stuff – what they had seen, what they had heard tell. Some of their tales made my hair stand on end, I can tell you! I met a sailor whose brother's cousin had seen furry men with heads like dogs. Another told me how, after three years at sea, he had sighted mermaids off the starboard bow. Mermaids! I told Sir John: 'Shouldn't you put that in your book?' But he just looked at me with that same odd look. 'Yes Clym, but is it TRUE?'

In the end, I collected my stories and he collected his. We would swap them at supper. He would tell me about some martyred virgin whose head flew away, and I would tell him about the anthropophagi who don't have heads at all but keep their faces in their chests. He would tell me about some caliph murdered by his wife, and I would tell him about green river-monsters in Egypt that pretend to be logs then swallow down whole boats.

His smile was always so *doubtful*. Once I banged the table with my fist and shouted, '*What, then, do all your fine clerics tell the truth and all my sailors tell lies?*'

Next moment, I was scared. A servant, shouting at his master? But Sir John, bless him, he just smiled and said, 'When we go there and see it, then I'll write it in my book.'

'Can we go, then? *Can* we? You know it said in your books that the world might be round? Well, we could go on and prove it. If we travelled round it, think what things you would have to write in your book! Folk would really want to read it, then!'

I can't think what made me say it. Already we had been travelling for two years, sleeping in pilgrims' hostels, camping under goatskins, sharing every plate of food with a swarm of flies. And here I was suggesting we go further, into unknown territories full of heathens whose skin wasn't even the same colour as mine. I must have gone mad.

Just for a moment, Sir John did seem to be tempted. Then he shook himself and poured another glass of wine. 'I'm a man of property, Clym. I have lands, family, responsibilities. I haven't got years to spend on madcap journeys round the world.'

My eyes filled with tears. I suppose Sir John thought I was mardy with disappointment, but actually I was remembering my plan.

I had meant, in some wild, out-of-the-way place, to cut his throat, put on his fine clothes, pocket all his letters of credit and go through the rest of life calling myself Sir John Mandeville. I had dreamed about it for months – how I would find some petty castle-court in France and marry some *duchesse* or *dauphinoise*, sending home to England once a year for more cash.

The world's a big place. Who would ever know?

But first I put it off because he was teaching me to read, then because he was teaching me Latin and Greek. And then somehow I got fond of him. I'd put off murdering him too long, you see? That night in the Sinai desert, I realised I was never going to do it: I had grown to love the man. I could no more cut his throat than catch a unicorn.

The night before we set sail for England, I got

talking to an old sea dog called Akbar. He wore his hair in a single grey plume rising from the top of his head. His face was pocky, missing an eye, and oddly reshaped by a set of home-made whalebone teeth. I told him about our travels in search of wonders, and of course that set Akbar talking.

'I've seen a place where lambs grow on trees, like fruit,' he said. 'I was shipwrecked on the Isle of Lodestone, which draws ships to it by the iron of their nails and wrecks them on its metal rocks! I've been to the country where each person has one great foot so large that he lies on his back in the shade of it.'

Mesmerised, spellbound, I watched those whalebone teeth clacking. Just for a second I found myself thinking, 'Yes, but is it TRUE?' Then I settled down to enjoy Akbar's stories, swallowing them down whole, like pilchards, between mugs of ale.

He had seen sea monsters, and lands where men and women go about stark naked; birds that talk and fish that glow in the dark. He had been in Borneo where jewels grow on the reed-stems. He fed me such a feast of facts, that when *he* started asking *me* questions, naturally I answered. I told him how Sir John was a prosperous gentleman, how we were setting sail next day, how we were sleeping in a store-room over the chandler's shop...

Sir John called me away then, or I would have talked more. My master said he had a present for me, so I instantly forgot Akbar and his tall tales.

It was a book. 'A gift for my loyal secretary, apt pupil and excellent good friend,' he said.

'*Me*, you mean?' I was soused with wine, and too astonished to be gracious. I cannot begin to imagine what he paid for a copy of John Plano Carpini. For *me*. For his excellent good friend!

'I am a poor adventurer, Clym,' he said. 'After two years, all I can think of is home and a yard of English ale. But you! You have the soul of a true explorer. Listen. If you want to go farther, go with my blessing. I free you from your employment. I'm sure I can weather one voyage on my own. Otherwise, come home to England with me, and sit in an armchair and read about the sights other valiant men put themselves to the pain of visiting. Eh, Clym? Which is it to be?'

My head was reeling. I could picture English orchards and Indian gems all at the same time; dog-headed men and Hertfordshire church steeples. 'May I tell you tomorrow?' I said, clutching the book to my chest.

We bedded down in that comfortless store-room over

the chandlery, surrounded by coils of rope, tackle, belaying pins and luggage, and went instantly to sleep.

I was woken by a single cry from Sir John.

The intruder was no more than a black shape amid the darkness, but as he turned for the door, I saw the flash of whalebone teeth, unnaturally white. And Sir John's money-belt in his fist. I tried to tackle him, but he lashed out, and I fell against the wall.

Sir John was dead before I reached him – a single stab wound through the heart. For the rest of the night I sat there beside him in the dark, crying. I remember wondering what part I ought to keep as a relic of this good, gentle, witty, clever man.

In the end, I kept his letters of credit, naturally.

That fool Akbar, being illiterate, had left the most valuable prize – the books. In the morning, I put on Sir John's clothes, packed up the diaries, his copy of Herodotus, Pliny and Friar Odoric, and as much luggage as I could carry. I went aboard the first ship to sail – bound not for England but for France. I called myself 'Sir John Mandeville, traveller and writer'. It was easy. Who in the world knew or cared enough to say any different?

*

That was thirty-four years ago. I am thinking to go home now – to St Albans, my home town. England is the best place to publish, the best place to grow old.

If my hands will let me, I'll just write the last line of this book of mine: *'I, John Mandeville, saw this, and it is the truth.'*

There now. The book is finished, and I venture to say there is no book like it in the world. Why did it take me so long to write? Well, an author must collect his material, mustn't he?

I've travelled halfway round the world – to Java and Sumatra, Ethiopia and India, Tibet and China and Tartary. I've lived in the palaces of emperors and dined on strange fish. And all the wonders I've seen are recorded here, in my life's work: *The Travels of Sir John Mandeville.* What? Why do you look at me like that?

Here you will read of men who are half-woman, of wilderness-people who grow horns and never speak, of giant snails and dog-headed men with tails, of lambs which grow on trees, and sons who cut off their father's heads at death to cook and eat; cyclopses with one eye set in their foreheads; Amazon warrior-women, and sultans who marry a dozen wives. Do you know, there is a forest of pepper trees in India twenty-three days long, and the kings there build castles on the backs of elephants?

Readers will gasp in amazement as they read, and wonder that the world can be so full of strangeness. Some will even ask, 'Yes, but is it TRUE?'

To them I say, 'Go and see for yourself! Why would I lie?'

Look at my hands – like two fistfuls of stones. I dropped the quill just now and it took me ten minutes to pick it up. I should employ a secretary, like that boy Clym so long ago in the Holy Lands. He looked a lot like me, they say: same ruddy complexion, same yellow ringlets. But he died young. Suddenly. I was there, and it was just as if he stepped through a door into another world, to see what new wonders it had to offer.

NOTE

The Travels of Sir John Mandeville, *a bestseller for centuries, has puzzled generations of scholars. Half seems to be genuine, the rest stitched together from sailors' stories, classical writings and other people's travel books. Some of the outlandish descriptions have a rational explanation – crocodiles, orangutans, howdahs, etc. – while others are purely absurd. Even so, world maps were redrawn on the strength of it. Leonardo da Vinci owned a copy. Christopher Columbus was inspired by it to attempt sailing round the world, and only gained the help of the King and Queen of Spain after they, too, had read Mandeville.*

So however much of the book was invented, it really did change the world.

15th
CENTURY

——————★——————

PETE JOHNSON

THE MYSTERY OF THE INVISIBLE FRIENDS

Illustrated by Mark Robertson

15th
CENTURY

PETE JOHNSON

THE MYSTERY OF THE INVISIBLE FRIENDS

I dare not say aloud what I have seen.

This is why I must write down exactly what happened on the night of August 21st 1485. I do not believe I shall ever set down anything which is more important – or more dangerous.

My name is John. I shall not give my other name in order to protect my parents' identity – and mine. I can tell you, though, that my parents are servants in the royal household.

They joined two years ago, shortly after King Edward IV had died. Everyone expected his son, also called Edward, to come to the throne. But he was only twelve and a half and Parliament wouldn't accept him as the new King. So his uncle, Richard III, had to reign in his place.

What happened to Prince Edward? Well, that was a real mystery. He just vanished. And no one knew where he'd gone. There were rumours that he and his younger brother, Richard, were living in the tower. I'd often hang about outside there in the hope of seeing the princes suddenly appear at a window. But they never did.

Once I did see someone enter the tower with a tray of food. I rushed up to him. 'Is that for the two princes? They're in the tower, aren't they?'

He didn't reply, just frowned hard and later reported what I'd said to my parents. They were furious with me.

'Do you want us to lose our positions here?' demanded my mother.

'Look, I only asked…'

'You must learn never to ask anything,' interrupted my father. Then he added, more gently, 'It is the only way to survive.'

A few days later I was in trouble again. I'd gone racing down one of the corridors (I can't remember why) when I crashed into someone heading in the opposite direction.

I heard the gasps of horror and shock first. Then I looked up. I'd only collided with the King. His face was thin, lined, and deathly pale – just his eyes seemed alive and alert. They were smiling faintly at me, even while he rubbed his shoulder.

My mother rushed forward apologising so fast I couldn't follow what she was gabbling about. I don't think the King could either. But he just looked at me and said, 'I believe all our enemies have flown.' Afterwards my mother told me that was a joke.

But sadly, the King's enemies hadn't all flown. 'This pack of Lancastrian rascals' (as my father calls them) had been organising uprisings against the Kings of England for over twenty years. The latest Lancastrian rascal was Henry Tudor.

'We have a good King who cares about all his subjects, rich and poor,' cried my mother. 'So why do the people want to follow this pretender to the throne?' But then she looked fearfully around her. Henry Tudor was rumoured to have spies everywhere.

The atmosphere at the palace was now very tense. King Richard had been away since May, and some people seemed to spend their whole day whispering gossip and rumours. Through these rumours, my parents heard the King was about to face Henry Tudor in a major battle.

On the night of August 21st I fell asleep, listening to them anxiously muttering about the King's chances in the battle ahead. Later that same night I started sleepwalking.

I have sleepwalked a number of times. But before, one of my parents had heard me and brought me back. Tonight, though, my weary parents heard nothing, while I walked on and on into the palace gardens.

A nightingale woke me up. It was singing its heart out. I stared around me. I had no idea where I was or how I had got here. I felt giddy and strange. I took some deep breaths. Then I saw I was not alone. A sword was hanging in the air right by my nose.

I gaped at it glinting in the moonlight. Then a voice said, 'What are you doing out here?'

I closed my eyes. If this was a dream I wanted to wake up fast. I opened my eyes again. To my horror nothing had changed. That sword was still ominously close to me.

'All right, if you won't answer – prepare to taste steel.'

I struggled to speak. But my lips were trembling too much.

Then a voice said, 'He's not an enemy. He's just a boy in his bed-clothes, he means us no harm. Put down your sword, Richard.' He spoke quietly but with authority.

And I managed to squeak, 'Truly, I do not mean you any harm.'

The sword was slowly drawn back. The two speakers swam into view. They were boys, not much bigger than me. I wondered what they were doing here. 'Do you... do you work in the stables?' I knew two boys had recently begun working there.

They just grinned at this. Then I noticed for the first time how well-dressed they were: both in blue velvet tunics with low hanging belts. The taller boy also had a magnificent chain around his neck. I'd never seen anything like it before. It was the kind of thing you imagine being worn by...

I blinked at them in astonishment. I must still have been dreaming. These figures would dissolve away any moment. This didn't make any sense. Suddenly my feet didn't seem to be touching the ground any more. I felt as if I was about to faint.

I stumbled forward. The taller of the boys put out his hand and held my arm.

'Are you all right?' he murmured.

'Yes, I think so,' I gasped. 'But are you really the Princes?'

The boy nodded gravely. 'I'm Prince Edward and this is my brother, Prince Richard.'

I attempted to bow. But immediately I felt giddy again. If Prince Edward hadn't kept a firm grasp on my arm I would have fallen right over.

'And who are you?' asked Prince Edward.

For one awful moment I couldn't think who I was. 'I'm John, Sire – and my mother and father are members of the royal household,' I added proudly.

Edward smiled. 'It is good to meet you, John. You are the first stranger we have spoken to in a long time.'

'Have you been living in the tower, then?' I asked.

'For two years now,' said Richard.

'And does your uncle force you to stay there so he can be King?'

Edward's face stiffened. 'Who said that?'

I lowered my head. 'Oh, just some people.'

'They have been listening to Lancastrian lies,' cried Edward. 'My uncle wanted me to be King. It was

Parliament who stopped me. My uncle very reluctantly had to rule in my place. But next year I come of age. Then he will make sure Parliament does not stop me again.'

'So you're a King-in-waiting,' I said.

Both the Princes liked that. The atmosphere relaxed again, and Prince Edward leant forward. 'Until I come of age I must wait in safety and secret. You see, Henry Tudor does not want me to be King. He feels I will reign for a long time. And he has followers everywhere.'

'Henry Tudor, that treble-dyed traitor!' Richard spat the words. 'I should like to pass this sword right through his heart.'

'If he has one,' I said.

'Well spoken,' said Richard, laughing.

'Do just the two of you live in that tower?' I asked.

'Yes' said Edward. 'But our tutor is there every day, and our mother is nearby. And it will not be for much longer. When my uncle defeats Henry Tudor, my brother and I can leave our fortress for ever.' His voice began to shake. He was tall but slightly built. And his face was nearly as pale and troubled as his uncle's. Richard was shorter but sturdier. His hair was jet black while Edward's was fair and wispy.

'Everyone expects the King to win,' I said.

'Our servants are not so certain,' replied Edward grimly. 'Two of them have disappeared.'

'They've run away,' said Richard contemptuously. 'So while our tutor slept we disobeyed orders and crept outside. You see, John, we're expecting an important message.' He looked at Edward as if to check he should go on. Edward gave a brief nod. Richard continued. 'Our uncle has been sending us messages in code. He does not think it is safe for us here any more. He wants us to stay in the North where he has many friends. So we are waiting for the signal to leave.'

I looked across the gardens as if expecting someone to spring out of the shadows. I saw the outline of an archway, and then I froze. In front of the archway was a hedge. And something in that hedge had just stirred. It was the tiniest movement. But something or someone was hiding there.

I hissed, 'Over in the hedge there, I saw someone move.'

Both the Princes started. Richard half-drew his sword. They peered ahead of them.

'I can't see anything,' whispered Richard, at last. 'Still, I ought to investigate.'

'No, it could be an assassin. Let me see who it is.' I was intoxicated by this meeting. I felt I could do anything. 'They won't be interested in me.'

Edward hesitated but Richard said, 'Be very careful though, Henry Tudor's men are ruthless. Just see if someone is there and then come right back. Do not try and fight them.'

He needn't have worried. I wasn't feeling quite that brave. I crept forward. The hedge loomed ahead. I squinted my eyes up. And then I saw a face stare back at me. It gave me the shock of my life.

It was an elderly man with a great bushy beard. He wasn't moving a muscle. He was lying in that hedge so still he could almost have been dead.

My heart thumping I rushed back to the Princes. I was in such haste that I caught my foot on a loose stone and stumbled towards them.

'Are you all right?' cried Edward.

'Yes, yes,' I said hastily. 'There is a man in that hedge, he's very old, with a really thick beard and...'

I saw the Princes smile with relief. Richard even gave a whistle of amusement.

'It is our tutor,' said Edward. 'He's noticed we've gone and he is keeping a watch on us. Poor Dr Alcock, we cannot leave him hiding in that hedge for much longer. Not at his age.'

Edward stretched out a hand to me. 'We must return to our fortress, but we will not forget you my friend, or the way you risked danger to help us tonight. "Loyalty binds me" – that is what my uncle says, and when I am King it will be my creed too.'

'Call on me any time,' I cried, shaking both their hands. 'And I hope your message arrives soon.'

Richard placed a finger over his mouth, but then whispered, 'So do we.'

I watched them move swiftly over to the hedge and help their tutor clamber out. Then with another wave they were gone.

I stood there, thinking over and over about what I'd seen. Not only had I spoken to the Princes, but I'd helped them a little – and they'd called me their friend.

Back in my bed I dreamt I was riding alongside the Princes and then King Richard appeared and gave me a sword as a reward for my loyalty.

I slept on. When I woke up a cold shiver ran through me. Right away I sensed something was wrong. Then I saw my parents sitting dejectedly together. They could hardly bear to tell me the news. King Richard had been betrayed by some of his followers. He had died honourably, in the thick of battle.

Henry Tudor was the new King. A mean, hawk-faced man whom my parents hated. But they still swore allegiance to him. They said they had no choice.

And soon Henry Tudor was spreading untruths about King Richard. He pretended King Richard had been a hunchback with a withered arm. And then he made up a truly vile lie: he said King Richard had killed his two nephews in the tower. He claimed the Princes had been dead for two years. I waited for someone to speak out against this evil falsehood – the Princes' mother, for instance. She knew the truth.

But suddenly, dramatically, Henry Tudor accused her of treachery and banished her to a convent. It caused quite a sensation. Dr Alcock, the Princes' tutor, was also denounced as a traitor. He vanished too.

Within days everyone who knew of the Princes' existence at the tower had disappeared, except me. I felt I had to speak out. Otherwise people would start to believe Henry Tudor's lies. I began by telling some of the servants what I'd seen on the night of August 21st.

That night my father struck me for the first time. 'If you go on telling that tale,' he cried, 'King Henry will have you hanged for treason, and your parents too. Is that what you want?'

Of course it wasn't. And in the end I stood up and retracted everything I'd said. My parents coached me. It was their idea to make me say the Princes were imaginary: two imaginary friends I'd created. I promised never to mention them again.

Every false word cut deep inside me. I'd betrayed the Princes. But no one could stop me thinking about them and wondering where they were.

I knew they hadn't been killed by King Richard. But had Henry Tudor murdered them? That was what my parents secretly thought. But surely not even Henry Tudor could have done that.

Of course the Princes might have escaped and been smuggled to safety. Were they hiding somewhere in the North now? I wished for that with all my heart. I wished to see them again too. But somehow I doubted that I ever would.

At night I would sit staring into the fire thinking and thinking about my invisible friends. One evening, my mother seeing me, came up and whispered, 'Remember, in the end truth is more powerful than any lie.'

That was all she dared say. How I hope she is right.

And one day you will be able to read my words without fear and know the truth about good King Richard III, and my friends, the two Princes.

16th
CENTURY

——————— ★ ———————

JACQUELINE WILSON

THE DAUGHTER

Illustrated by Sarah Young

Jacqueline Wilson

The Daughter

I turn the handle of the spit. Turn and turn and turn. The fat from the fowl spatters my face. The great fire scorches me until I am half-cooked myself.

I turn and turn and turn though my back is breaking, turn though my hands are blistered. My mouth is so dry I can barely swallow but I finished my mug of small beer an hour ago. I am so weary that my eyes start closing, c-l-o-s-i-n-g...

'Keep turning, you useless feeble girl!' roars the Master Meat Cook.

The other scullions snigger.

The Cook is kind to the boys. He gives them the choicest left-overs and when they've done their chores he joins them in their games of football in the gardens.

The Cook throws the blown-up pig's bladder at my head, knocking me smartly so that my eyes sting.

'There! That will wake you up,' says the Cook.

He hates me. He hates me even though I am his daughter, his only child. He hates me *because* I am his daughter, his only child. He hates me because I killed my mother.

She was the Sweetmeat Cook. When my father speaks of her he savours her name as if her own rosewater candies were melting on his tongue. They were brought up together in the Palace kitchens, childhood sweethearts. They wed when they came of age and were delighted when my mother grew big with child. A lusty boy to follow in his father's footsteps in the Palace.

But I was a girl, a red-faced bawling babe who nearly tore my mother apart. She took me in her arms at last and I stared at her with my great green eyes.

'Witch's eyes,' says my father, spitting. 'You looked at your mother and put a curse on her. She died of a fever three days after.'

He's never said it, but I know he wishes I'd died too. But he paid for me to be brought up in the village, and when I was six he took me to live with him inside the Palace. Not as his child. As the junior scullion. To scrub and scrape and steep – and to turn and turn and turn the spit for the roasting meat. Boar and beef, capons, pheasants, quails and swans.

When Father thwacks the sides of meat with his axe his face is contorted and I jump at each thud. When he skewers each limp bird body I tremble. When he chops off a head I shut my eyes tight.

I have to scurry round and sweep up the eyes and beaks, the paws and claws, the reeking ribbons of innards. Once I saved two severed swan's wings and tried to work out how to fix them to my back so I could fly far away. The wings withered and started to smell and I had to throw them on to the rubbish heap. I tried straddling the kitchen broom but my feet stayed flat on the floor. My father thinks me a witch but I see no evidence of any magic powers, black or white.

I pretend though. It's the only way I can stop the other scullions making my life even more of a misery. When their pokes and prods become too vicious I raise my head and stare straight at them, widening my eyes until they water.

'Lizzie's giving us the witch's eyes!' they say, giggling nervously. 'Foolish girl! Can't scare us.'

But they back away, ducking their heads, out of my line of sight. I scare them all right.

I once tried the eye trick on Father, when I caught him in the corner with the Pudding Cook, the woman who was once my poor dead mother's friend. I thought of Mother underneath the cold earth, eternally unembraced. I widened my eyes – and Father saw me over her shoulder.

He hit me then. He beat me until neither of my witch's eyes could open and for days the kitchen was a blur.

Turn and turn and turn. The spit is chock-a-block with flesh and fowl and there's still a vast heap of dead creatures waiting in the wet room. We are preparing for a huge celebratory banquet. The new Queen has withdrawn to her chambers and started her labours at dawn today. We are all awaiting the birth of the little Prince.

In the cool at the far end of the kitchen the Sugar Cook has fashioned a sugar cradle that really rocks and now he is modelling a marchpane babe, its head eerily real, its arms and legs neatly tucked up, its bare bottom on show for all to gawp at.

'And if it's a girl they can always pull off its twiddly bit,' one of the scullions giggles.

The Sauce Cook hits him with her ladle and my father frowns. It is not a laughing matter. The King has to have a son and heir. That is why he discarded the first Queen and little Princess. Now he has the new Queen, the one they whisper is also a witch. She has certainly bewitched the King, but so long as she gives birth to a fine healthy son she will need no magic charms.

It will be a son. The finest astrologers in the land have consulted their charts and declared it to the King. The Royal Physicians have prodded the Queen beneath her farthingale and agreed that the unborn infant is definitely a male child. The Queen's Ladies have performed all the usual tests and tricks and each and every time they are united in their testimony: a boy.

The Palace is agog with the good news – but as the hours progress there is a growing tension. The Queen's chambers are at the other end of the Palace, but every now and then I fancy I can hear her high-pitched screams.

I turn and turn and turn, the fire slow smouldering for the swan and turkey, but banked up to roaring heat to crisp the pork and sear the game birds.

As the hours pass the tensions worsen in the kitchen. Every table is covered with cooked meats, glistening gold and ruby red and rich brown – but maybe this is a banquet that will never be touched.

The new Queen has been in hard labour for too long. The Pudding Cook scurries the corridors and whispers with her friends in the bed chambers. She tells us that they've sent for the local Wise Woman.

'But she's a witch, everyone knows that!' my father gasps.

'A witch to help a witch,' says the Pudding Cook. 'She knows a secret trick of speeding labour.'

The Wise Woman works her magic charms. Just after four the Pudding Cook comes speeding back down the corridors.

'The babe is born! Alive and well – and the Queen too, though exhausted.'

'The King has his son!' my father shouts, punching the air with his fist, and the kitchen rocks with hurrahs.

'No! No, it is a daughter, a girl!' says the Pudding Cook.

There's a sudden appalled silence.

My father stares at me, his old sorrow sharpening his face.

'Turn!' he shouts.

I turn and turn and turn, eyes lowered, because I do not want another beating.

I roast the bird, though the banquet will be a sad affair. The Sweetmeat Cook mutilates his marchpane babe, decides it is too cruel a reminder, and starts to mix a vat of sugar and eggwhite, intent on wrapping the child with edible swaddling.

There's an order from the King! We are all allowed extra ale to drink the health of the Queen and her new child. Doubtless it would have been fine wine if a boy had been born. But the ale is welcome nonetheless, and the kitchen is soon a merry place for all but me. My father allows the scullions their share of ale too, but I am only permitted my usual small beer which fails to flush the cheeks or fuddle the brain.

My father is very flushed, very fuddled. He is fooling with the Pudding Cook, dipping his finger in syrup, writing sticky messages on her bare neck. But then word is sent from the Queen's chambers. Her Majesty is reviving and requires a good posset curd to build up her strength.

The Pudding Cook panics and gets to work with a great clattering of pans. She needs to seethe her milk on the fire so she elbows me out of the way. She starts cracking the eggs in her mixture, one after another, beating clumsily. Her face is red with effort, her hair hanging in her eyes. She fails to stir enough, and the fire is too fierce.

'It's curdling!' she wails. 'It's ruined!'

She turns to me. 'It's all your fault! You put the evil eye on it. You're a child of the Devil.'

She strikes at me with her spoon. I dodge, my arms flailing – and knock her whole bowl flying across the floor. She hits me again, knocking me over, so I roll into the fire, the fire, the fire...

My hands, my hands! But someone is soothing them with cool lotion and wrapping them in soft linen, singing to me gently all the while. Is it my mother? Have I died and gone to Heaven?

I open my eyes. I stare at two orbs as green as my own – but this is an old woman with wrinkles deep in her face and silver hair. She smiles at me, and I smile back in spite of the pain.

'Your daughter will recover,' she says over her shoulder.

'Thank you for your help, Wise Woman,' the Pudding Cook mumbles, chastened.

'I doubt her hands will heal though. She'll be good

for nothing if she cannot turn that spit,' says my father. 'What use will the girl be then?'

'She would be of use to me. I have need of an apprentice,' says the Wise Woman. 'Pray let me take your daughter, Master Cook. I will give you a good price for her.'

She tips out half the purse of gold given to her by the Queen. My father does not argue. He stoops and gathers the coins before she can change her mind.

'You gave that vast sum for *me*!' I whisper, stunned, as she leads me away from the Palace on her old mare.

'Your father certainly does not hold you dear!'

'It is because I am evil. I killed my mother,' I confess. 'My father said that I stared at her with my green witch's eyes the day I was born and put a curse on her.'

'What nonsense,' says the Wise Woman, tucking her own shawl about my shoulders. 'All newborn babes have *blue* eyes. I of all women should know that.'

I can scarcely absorb this information.

'Even so,' I whisper, 'why should you waste a fortune on a useless girl-child?'

'Girls are of great value,' says the Wise Woman. 'We are entering a new age. The little red-haired babe born today will make a fine Queen of England.'

She wraps the shawl tight, like mock swaddling.

'And you shall be *my* babe, my little witch daughter – and one day you will be as wise a woman as me.'

17th
CENTURY

———— ★ ————

JEREMY STRONG

LONDON RISES FROM THE ASHES
(and how it nearly all went wrong)

Illustrated by Tim Stevens

JEREMY STRONG

LONDON RISES FROM THE ASHES
(and how it nearly all went wrong)

The streets of London were still smouldering even though many days had passed since the Great Fire had given its final flicker. The ground, two foot deep in some places with ash and embers, was hot to walk on. Titus Drumm danced and jigged as he made his way along all that was left of Snout Lane, his gorgeous lace-frilled cuffs flopping about his hands like a host of attendant doves.

'Oh! Ouch!' The charcoal had burned through the

soles of both boots, his *best* boots no less. Titus was not simply in pain; he was cross. He could not find the house he was looking for (because it had burnt to the ground along with everything else), and now he could not remember *who* he was looking for.

Titus danced up the road, sweating beneath his heavy wig, trying to recall what His Majesty King Charles II had told him. His Royal Highness was most anxious to rebuild the city. Most of London had gone up in flames, including the great church of St Paul. King Charles wanted it replaced, at once.

'The people must see that we are repairing the city. There is no time to be lost. I want every new building made from stone or brick – anything that won't catch fire. My tailor's shop was almost consumed by flames – a near disaster! Get Christopher Wren to draw up plans and start work immediately,' the King had boomed from on high (he was six foot two inches tall), before turning back to the large gilt mirror in order to admire his new silk hosiery and fabulously huge hat. 'Now I must be off to see that woman who has such nice oranges.'

'Yes Sire, at once Sire,' Titus had beamed as he reversed, bowing and scraping and tripping over his own lace boot tops. He had silently cursed the frothy garters. French they might be. Fashionable they might be. But they weren't much good if they were liable to break a man's neck.

Now Titus pranced up Snout Lane and tried to remember the name of England's great architect. 'Oh la-de-dah, I know it was a bird,' he muttered. 'Christopher Robin? Owl? Wagtail? Corncrake? What was it?'

All around him ragged figures poked amongst the ruins of buildings. A few carts, laden with rescued belongings, jerked and jolted past him, the horses pulling with bowed heads. The stench of burnt wood, burnt cloth, burnt fur and burnt skin filled the dark air. A dishevelled figure detached itself from the smoking skeleton of a house. The woman's face, arms and dress were all smeared with soot where she had been grovelling amongst the remains of her charred home.

'Good woman,' called Titus. 'Does not England's greatest architect live near here?'

'Oh my, it's Lord High-an'-Mighty 'imself. I don't know of no great arky-whatsit. Look.' The woman thrust a small bit of blackened wood into Titus's face. 'Know what that is?'

'Indeed I don't.'

'Knock on it,' she commanded. 'Go on. Knock on it.'

Titus felt a trifle embarrassed, but he rapped the little piece of wood with his knuckles.

'Come in,' beamed the woman, grinning madly at him.

'What?'

'Come in! That's my front door that is, what you's knockin' on. All that's left of it. Come in!'

'I'm sorry,' mumbled Titus.

'Don't matter,' said the woman matter-of-factly. 'Ain't no house for it to stick on anyways.'

Titus tried again. 'I'm looking for a man who designs things; goes by the name of a bird. Christopher something-or-other.'

'Ah,' mused the woman, 'that'll be Mister Thrush.'

'That's it!' cried Titus, at once forgetting his burning feet. 'Thrush! Does he live near by?'

'He would if he could.'

'What do you mean by that?'

'I mean that this was 'is house, an' a flea would be hard-pressed to live in it now, what with the state it's in, an' I can tell you we weren't short of fleas afore the fire. 'Ad enough fleas to stuff a pillow, so the lodger told me, an' he 'ad the bites to prove it an 'all.' The grimy woman fixed Titus with one eye. 'I am Mistress Jellicoe sir, Mr

Thrush's servant, what does 'is cookin' an' cleanin' an' chamberpot emptyin' an' such. If you want the master you'll have to go to The Beggar's Armpit. It's about the only tavern still standin' around here.'

Titus fiddled in his purse and produced a silver sovereign. 'Thank you, thank you my good woman!' he cried, and he strode off toward the tavern.

Mistress Jellicoe watched him disappear, tested the coin on her black teeth and carried on muttering. 'I ain't a good woman, not good at all. I put a mouse in Mr Thrush's soup once… an' it couldn't swim.'

The Beggar's Armpit was in one of the few areas that had escaped the Great Fire, tucked down a dingy alleyway that stank of rotting food and emptied chamberpots. The old wooden houses were so ancient that they actually appeared to be propping each other up, like crumbling crones no longer able to stand on their own feet. Now the tavern itself was seething with refugees from the fire: noisy men and rowdy women and slopping ale.

Christopher Thrush – designer, inventor and possible genius – sat in the dingiest corner, cursing his luck. His house had burnt down before his eyes, along with his latest invention, the world's first dishwasher, almost completed. It would have made him rich and famous. Now he had nothing. He buried his pinched face in his leather tankard and sipped the dregs of beer, wishing that he was dead.

It was at this moment of deepest despair that a vision appeared before him, a vision that came in the portly, lace be-ribboned shape of Titus Drumm. The King's messenger bowed low, pulled forward a stool, parked his ample backside upon it and beamed at Christopher.

'Mr Thrush? I am here on a mission from His Majesty the King. He requires you to oversee the rebuilding of London, and he wishes you to commence work on the new church of St Paul at once.'

Christopher Thrush was so astonished that the first thing he did was punch Titus hard on the nose. The poor messenger tumbled backwards into a pool of spilled cider. At once Christopher was on his feet, helping the dazed man rise from the filthy rush floor and brushing down his ornate doublet. Christopher seized the messenger's wig from the puddle, squeezed half a pint of old cider from the wool ringlets and carefully arranged it back on Titus's shaven pate. Bits of rush poked out from beneath.

'I am so very sorry sir, but in my misery I thought you must be a dream that had come to taunt me. Now I see the blood pouring out of your nose I realise that you are indeed flesh and – well, blood indeed. Is this your tooth on the floor? My dear sir, this is wonderful news. The King really wants *me*?'

'Indeed,' grunted Titus, dabbing his nose with his perfumed hanky. 'You are to start work at once.'

Christopher's head almost spun with joy and invention. The buildings he would erect! The houses! The churches! His brain seethed with fabulous creations, and the most remarkable of all was the new church of St Paul. All night long he sketched his design. By the time morning came he had the plans for the most extraordinary church England would ever see.

Christopher hurried out into the early morning air, still carrying the stink of charred wood, and hailed a passing sedan chair. 'Take me to Titus Drumm!' cried the genius, waving his master plan at the two ragged carriers. 'I am going to save London!'

One of the men glanced ruefully at the smouldering houses all around. 'What are you going to do?' he asked. 'Wee on it?'

But Christopher was already clambering into the

sedan. A moment later he was hoisted into the air and the carriers were off at a gangly gallop. Inside, Christopher was bumped up and down and hurled about in general, but he was far too excited to notice. His plan for St Paul's was a masterpiece.

Unfortunately Titus Drumm didn't agree. Titus studied the plan from every angle and at last he made an observation. 'La-de-dah,' he sighed. 'It's round, like a pig's bladder for playing football.'

'A ball, like the earth,' explained Christopher. 'The new church is like a model of God's earth itself.'

'But there are no windows,' Titus growled. 'How does any light pierce the gloom of this earth of yours?'

'Ah! That's one of my surprises – there *is* no roof! Light comes pouring straight in from above.'

'But so will the rain,' Titus pointed out. 'The congregation won't like getting wet.'

'Ah!' cried Titus again. 'The rain won't fall on them. It will fall upon the Garden of Eden.'

'Really?' Titus was beginning to look round for help, for someone who would rescue him from this madman. In the depths of his mind a suspicion was beginning to stir. Christopher THRUSH?

'Yes,' Christopher went on eagerly. 'Inside the globe

is a miniature Garden of Eden, raised upon marble pillars – a real garden, like a miniature forest, with plants and trees and all flowering things. There will be tigers roaming and elephants and...'

'Tigers and elephants roaming in the church! La-de-dah!' Titus clutched a chair for support.

'... and monkeys in the trees and great pythons and bats and birds of all kinds: parrots and humming birds, penguins, giant ostriches, the tiny wren...'

'WREN!' yelled Titus Drumm. Of course – Christopher *Wren*! Relief flooded through him. Hurrah! He pulled a purse full of sovereigns from his pocket and thrust it into Christopher's surprised hands. 'Here, take this money and your plan and go away. It won't do. The King doesn't want elephants and monkeys. Go, go!'

Even as he spoke, Titus was pushing Christopher out. A moment later the door slammed on the inventor and he was left standing bewildered on the street.

Christopher Thrush trudged wearily back towards The Beggar's Armpit, once again in despair. But the nearer he came to the tavern the more he brightened up. He had a full purse of silver in his pocket. He could begin work on that amazing new invention of his again. He would be famous and rich...

17

So it was that while Sir Christopher Wren got to work on the new St Paul's Cathedral, Christopher Thrush got back to work on the world's first dishwasher. It looked like a wardrobe sitting on the back of a cart, harnessed to two horses. This was because it *was* a wardrobe sitting on the back of a cart, harnessed to two horses.

Christopher opened the wardrobe door to show puzzled onlookers the inside. 'My servant Mrs Jellicoe has placed all the dirty porcelain, all the filthy pots and pans inside here,' he explained, pointing at the packed shelves. 'On top is a tank of clean, hot water. I shut the door and pull this chain so...'

There was a gurgle and gush as the tank emptied into the wardrobe. A few drops leaked out through the door.

'The dishwasher is now ready.'

Christopher took the leading horse by the reins and walked it up the mud-rutted road. 'As the dishwasher passes over the bumps in this road the pots and pans are shaken about in the water until they are quite clean,' he shouted above the clattering noise from inside. 'This saves everyone a great labour. And now the washing is done. Behold!' He flung wide the wardrobe door.

To avoid embarrassing Christopher Thrush any further the recounting of this story concludes here.

18th
CENTURY

———★———

ADÈLE GERAS

TOINETTE

Illustrated by Sarah Young

Adèle Geras

Toinette

'Sit there, Toinette, and don't say a word. Pretend you're a little dog on a velvet cushion.' Rose lifted her sister on to the window sill.

'What colour should I be?'

'Black. A lap dog like the ones the ladies carry round in their arms. In winter they put them in their muffs.'

'I want to be golden brown.' Toinette was beginning to pout.

'Be any colour you like. Only be very, very quiet and

don't move because if I don't finish making this bit of lace, Madame will throw us into the street and we won't have anywhere to live.'

That silenced the little girl.

Rose sighed and turned to the cushion on which her piece of lace was taking shape: snowflakes and leaves and little lines of holes in a pattern so dense and intricate that it made you dizzy just to look at it. It was all in a fine silk thread that was hard on the eyes, which was why Rose had to hurry. Once the daylight was gone, that was that. No candles were to be burned, by order of Madame.

Madame sounded fiercer than she really was. After all, Rose reminded herself, if it hadn't been for her, both of us would be dead. Me and poor Toinette, who's only five.

The rest of the family she tried not to think about, for they were all in the ground, but as she worked, she remembered the muddy streets of her village and their own dark cottage. And the family…

The baby was first to die. Then Gran'père and Gran'mère. Then Maman. There was no food, none at all, and the winter of 1788 was the hardest anyone had seen for years and years. They said that wolves came into towns from the forest, because they were as starved as the people. No one dared leave a small child playing by itself. Rose thought of her father. No one knew where he'd gone. He'd simply disappeared. She couldn't recall what he looked like, but he used to say: 'These taxes will kill us.' Rose never knew what taxes were, and thought of them as huge, red, skinny spider-like creatures who lived under the bed and came out at night. Now that she was more grown-up (she would be eleven soon) she knew they were nothing but money that you had to pay to the King.

'Everything is changing now,' Madame said. 'People are saying that everyone will be equal... Imagine that! I don't for one moment believe it, but that's what I hear... Peasants and workers will be the same as aristocrats, and my customers won't be any finer than I am... But until that happens, my girl, you must apply yourself to your lace, because there's one thing sure: ladies will always want pretty things, whether they're princesses or serving-girls.'

I'm fortunate, Rose thought, looking at her sister. Toinette had decided being a cat was better because you could lick your hands, and also purr from time to time. The nuns in the village had somehow known – perhaps an angel had told them – that Rose had what M'sieur le Curé called 'silver fingers', and they had trained her well to make lace and embroider. And when all the others were dead, Sœur Cécile had given her a letter addressed to Madame in Paris.

Rose and Toinette had left the village carrying a small bundle of food and old clothes that the convent had given them. Fortunately the village was only two days' walk from Paris.

'My second cousin writes,' Madame said, when she saw them, 'that you are alone in the world. Also that you can make lace. She asks me to find a place for you here, in my workshop. I can ill afford it, but if you are as gifted as she says... And what about her?' She pointed, rather rudely, at Toinette.

'She's my sister,' Rose said, and was about to launch into a speech about how good Toinette was, and how she would look after her all the time, but a better idea occurred to her. 'I'm teaching her to embroider. She will be very skilful.'

Madame sniffed. 'Very well. You may both stay. These are troubled times. You must work hard. The ladies who buy my gloves and shawls and collars are the highest, the *very* highest in the land.'

Rose had nearly finished the piece. Soon, she'd be able to make breathtaking lace like *La Silencieuse*, the Silent One, who kept to herself up in the attic and made the most important pieces. Colette, Angèle and Germaine, who worked in the same room as she did, had gone to collect parcels of fabric from the merchant. Rose liked them because they all loved Toinette, and spoiled her, and sometimes gave her little gifts. Chocolate was best, from the shop in the next street. Sometimes, the fragrance of the sweet, dark stuff came floating over the rooftops and into the room where they worked.

Now here was Madame in a fluster. Her cheeks were red and she was wearing her best bonnet.

'Where is everyone?' she asked, and then remembered that she'd sent them out herself. She sighed and said to Rose, 'You'll have to do. Come with me. I need someone to carry the boxes. Put down your work and go and make yourself presentable. The carriage will be here directly. And I suppose we can't leave the little one alone here. Take her with you and wash her hands.'

'My hands are clean,' Toinette said. 'I've been licking them. Look.'

Madame wrinkled her nose. 'Wash them *thoroughly*,' she told Rose. 'And hurry. A carriage has been sent.'

The inside of the carriage was beautiful. The seats were blue velvet and the door handles were painted gold. Four gleaming brown horses pulled it along, and their hooves rang on the cobbles.

'Where are we going?' Rose asked.

'To Versailles,' Madame said. 'The Queen herself – imagine that! – has asked to see some samples, and if she likes them, why, that'll be the making of us. You girls must sit quite silently and wait till we are called.'

Rose thought the heart would burst out of her chest, it was beating so loudly.

'We're going to see the Queen,' she whispered to Toinette. 'In a palace?'

'Oh, yes! The most wonderful palace in the world – just like something from a story.'

Nothing Rose had imagined prepared her for the magnificence of Versailles. They were put to wait in a room with polished wooden floors and seats upholstered in scarlet brocade. There were grandly dressed people everywhere, and Rose thought they must be princes and princesses until Madame told her they were the palace servants. There was a painting all over the ceiling and Rose was so busy craning her neck to look at it that she didn't notice her sister wandering away down a long corridor.

'Where is the little one?' Madame asked suddenly. 'You were supposed to be looking after her... Do I really have to do every single thing myself? Go and find her this instant. Go on. Quickly.'

Rose was cold all over. Where could Toinette be? And

how was she supposed to find her in this place with its hundreds of rooms, each one bigger than the cottage she was born in? She couldn't shout – you didn't shout in a palace, she was quite sure of that. But could you run? Along those endless passages and through the galleries? I don't care, Rose thought. She's my sister. I must find her.

She ran through room after room, not noticing the heavy velvet curtains at the windows, nor the tall mirrors reflecting the June sky.

'Toinette!' she called. 'Where are you? Where have you hidden yourself?'

'She's in here,' said a pleasant voice. 'With me.'

Rose followed the voice into a room. There was her sister, sitting on the lap of a lady wearing a black dress in spite of the warm weather. The room was a bedroom, and Rose couldn't take her eyes off the bed: a gigantic four-poster hung with brocade curtains. A whole family could have slept in it, with space left over for the dog.

'I'm so sorry, Madame,' said Rose, curtseying. 'She's only five...'

Toinette jumped off the lady's lap. 'I said I was five. This lady asked me to come in.'

'That's quite true. I did. She reminded me...'

The lady turned away. She was drying her eyes with a

handkerchief. Rose thought: if I had a bedroom like this, I wouldn't feel like crying.

'You must forgive me,' the lady said. 'My baby – my son – died not more than two weeks ago. I find the world a little difficult at the moment, and your sister is just the age he was. Her chatter pleased me.'

Rose shivered because the lady looked at her with just the same sorrowful expression in her eyes as Maman had when they told her about Bébé.

'Our baby brother died when he was tiny,' she said. It was the first time she had spoken of this to anyone. 'Also the rest of our family. We had no food and no money to pay taxes.'

The lady said nothing, but shook her head sadly and said something under her breath that Rose couldn't hear. Then she stood up.

'I have to go now,' she said. 'Someone has come all the way from Paris to show me some samples of lace.'

'That's Madame Desmartins,' Rose said. 'We came with her. I'm one of her lacemakers.'

'Then let us go and find her together,' said the lady. 'But before we do, I must give this little one something to remember me by.' She looked around, and then picked up an enamelled box that stood on the mantelpiece and held it out to Toinette. 'This is pretty, isn't it? Look, it has a picture of a

shepherd and shepherdess on it.'

'Where are the lambs?'

The lady laughed. 'You're quite right, my darling. There should be lambs, indeed there should. Let's pretend the lambs have all been taken back to the barn, shall we?'

'Yes,' said Toinette. 'They've gone to sleep.'

'Exactly,' said the lady. 'Now come along with me.'

Toinette held on to her box and kept looking at it, even as they walked along the corridors.

'I forgot to ask your names,' the lady said. 'How impolite of me.'

'I'm Rose, and my sister is Toinette.'

'Is that short for Antoinette?'

Rose nodded, and the lady laughed again and clapped her hands.

'That's my name too,' she said.

'My sister was named for the Queen,' said Rose.

'I'm the Queen,' said the lady. 'Marie Antoinette. And I'm honoured to have such a pretty little girl named for me.'

She knelt down and kissed Toinette on both cheeks. Toinette flung her arms round the lady's – the Queen's – neck and clung to her as though she never wanted to let go. When the Queen stood up again, Rose saw that there were tears in her eyes. Her voice trembled a little as she said:

'Time to go and find Madame Desmartins. I'm so pleased she brought you both. You're a good sister, I can see that. How old are you, my dear?'

'I'm ten,' Rose said, 'but I'll be eleven soon.'

They had come to the place where Madame was waiting, and Rose knew that she wanted to be cross but couldn't be, because of the Queen.

'These children have lightened my day a little, Madame,' the Queen told her. 'Thank you for bringing them.'

On the way back to Paris, Toinette slept. Rose looked out of the carriage window and noticed suddenly how thin and poor and dirty all the people were who stood at the side of the road and watched the splendid carriage passing by. She thought of the palace, and the chandeliers hanging from the ceiling like complicated arrangements of stars. It wasn't right that some people lived in fine palaces, and others died of hunger. Perhaps it would change.

Rose closed her eyes and turned her thoughts to her

birthday. Not long to wait now. She would be eleven years old on the fourteenth of July.

NOTE

On July 14th 1789, the Bastille Prison in Paris was stormed. This event is usually considered to be the beginning of the French Revolution.

19th
CENTURY

———— ★ ————

MALORIE BLACKMAN

NORTH

Illustrated by David Wyatt

MALORIE BLACKMAN

NORTH

'That child of yours able to breed yet?'

'No, sir.'

'You sure? She started her monthlies?'

'No, sir.' Mama shook her head. 'She's only a baby.'

Best Friend grabbed at my face with one of his pudgy, doughy hands. He squeezed my cheeks together until my eyes started to water. He turned my face this way and that as he looked me up and down.

'She ain't no baby.' Best Friend pushed me away and

wiped his hand on his waistcoat. 'The minute she's old enough to breed, I've got someone ready to buy her.'

'Mama...'

'Hush, child.' Mama quietened me down at once.

I glared up at Best Friend. How could he take me from my mama? How would he feel if someone took his own daughter Amelia away from him? But as far as Best Friend and all the other whites up at the house were concerned, us slaves didn't have no feelings. I hated him so much that sometimes I thought I'd fill the whole world up with hate.

Best Friend's eyes began to narrow as he looked at me and I knew my face was showing too much. I blanked my expression and looked down at the dirt.

'I want to know the moment she's got the curse. D'you hear, Abby?'

'Yes, sir,' Mama replied.

Best Friend stomped back to the house. Mama had sure got his name right. He was the best friend of the Devil and no mistake. I waited until he was safely in the house before turning round.

'Mama, you're not going to let him sell me, are you? You can't.'

Mama carried on staring up at the house.

'Mama?'

'Hush, child. Come along now. We've got work to do and I don't fancy no back-whipping just 'cause you've got it in your head to ask questions.'

'I won't go. I won't. He can't make me,' I shouted.

'Child, hold your noise,' Mama warned.

'I won't go, d'you hear? And if you let him take me then you're... you're nothing but a coward and a...'

Mama slapped me so hard, my head snapped back.

'That's enough of your foolishness,' Mama hissed. 'Now get back to work on those vegetables, you hear?'

Mama moved off towards the side of the house. Tears swam into my eyes and down my cheeks as I watched her move away. And just at that moment, I hated her. I hated her for giving in, for saying 'Yes, sir' and 'No, sir' all the time. I hated her for being a slave. I hated her because I was her daughter and that made me a slave too and I would've chosen to be any number of other things – even Best Friend's worst kept dog – before I was a slave.

I went to work tending to the vegetables, wondering what I should do. Best Friend didn't know it yet but I was already seeing the curse. I'd had the curse for almost three months now. It was only a matter of time before he got to find out and then I'd be sold to the highest bidder faster than I could spit. But what could I do? As I dug around the carrots and potatoes, I turned over and over in my mind all the things I could do to get away. I turned my head this way and that, wondering which way I'd have to go to be free. Which was the right direction? All the ways looked the same. There were no paths leading away. Each road just led back to Best Friend's door.

A cool, hard hand clamped over my mouth. My eyes opened that same second.

'Hhmmm! Ugghh!' I struggled against the hand. My hands flew upwards to pull it off my mouth.

'Shush!' Mama's voice was barely a whisper. 'Shush! We're going North.'

We're going North.

You can have no idea what those few words did to me. I was that instant awake, as if a bucket of winter water had been tipped all over me. I was scared. More than scared. Terrified. But I was happy. Fiercely, raging happy. We were leaving. We were going to run away. And where were we going?

North.

North meant freedom. North was the closest thing on God's earth to Heaven. My eyes were getting used to the moonlit darkness. I smiled at Mama. She didn't smile back. Instead her eyes burnt into mine, shining hot and bright as the very sun itself.

Mama took hold of my hand as I sat up, and we tiptoed past the others in our shack who lay on sacking on the floor. I could hear folks sighing and some were even crying in their sleep. As we approached, Old John who lay in the middle of the shack started coughing, that terrible hacking, bone-shaking cough of his. I'm used to him coughing himself to sleep and then coughing himself awake again, but at that moment I was terrified he was going to wake up the whole world. Mama led the way towards the door. Old John hacked so bad, he started to sit up. Mama froze, her grip on my hand tightening. I didn't even dare to breathe. Old John didn't hold with folks running off. He said it was useless, a waste of time and just made life harder for everyone else.

As if life could get any harder.

Old John gave one final cough and collapsed back down on to his bedding. Immediately Mama pulled me towards the door. I almost stepped on Old John's foot – more in spite than anything else – but I wanted to go North, more than I wanted to get back at him for almost ruining our escape.

At last we were at the door. Mama opened it and for once it didn't squeak.

'Mama...?'

'I oiled it. Shush!'

And then we were outside. In the warm, night-time air. It had never felt so good on my face. The full moon shone like new money, but beneath the trees, where the moonlight didn't reach, there was pure darkness. I mean, darkness thick enough to almost drink.

'Sit.' Mama pushed down on one of my shoulders.

I sat down with a bump. After another quick glance around, then up at the house, Mama dug into her sack and took out two rolled up squares of rawhide and tied them to my feet using some rope. There was something slippy in the rawhide that made my toes curl. Then Mama sat and tied two larger squares of rawhide on to her own feet. She jumped up, pulling me up after her. Across the way I could see Best Friend's house. A single light shone in an upstairs window. Mama looked at it too, a cold, hard look on her face. She pulled me in the opposite direction towards the trees. And we started running.

We ran and ran and ran until I thought I was going to throw up my whole insides all over my rawhide shoes.

'Mama, can we stop?' I panted.

'No, child. Not yet.'

We ran and ran and ran some more. My legs felt burning hot, melting my bones away to nothing.

'Mama, I need to stop. My legs hurt. My chest is burning.'

'No child. Not yet.'

We ran until I fell to the ground, weeping.

'Mama, I can't go on no more. I can't.'

Mama squatted down in front of me, cupping my face in both her hands. 'Child, we'll rest for five minutes then we must keep moving. We have a long way to go before we reach the Ohio River.'

'And what happens then?'

'We cross the river and then we'll be north. Not North where we'll be free, but north where we should be safe. And then we'll just keep going north until we're free as the wind.'

I rubbed the rawhide covering my feet. The soles of my feet felt slippery and sore.

'What's in this rawhide, Mama?'

'Lard, pepper and some strong-smelling herbs.'

'Why?'

'To throw off the dogs. The minute Best Friend finds out we've gone, he'll be after us with every dog he's got.'

'It ain't right to set dogs on people.' I shook my head.

'Child, a lot of things in this world ain't right. You change them and fix them or you just put up with them.'

'We can't change anything, Mama. We're just slaves.'

'Uh-uh! No!' Mama shook her head. 'Just 'cause white folks say we're only fit to be slaves, don't make it so – don't make it *true*.'

'Maybe we're fixing things by… by running away?'

'Maybe we are at that.' A trace of a smile played across Mama's face.

I bowed my head and sighed. 'I'm sorry for what I said this afternoon. I didn't mean it.'

'I know that.' Mama sat next to me on the dry, cool ground and gathered me into her arms. 'And I'm sorry I slapped you. But I reckon I was so angry 'cause I thought maybe you was right.'

I was shocked. 'You ain't no coward, Mama. The Devil's Best Friend is the coward, whipping us and starving us and worse. He ain't no kind of man. Not as I would describe it, anyways.'

Mama laughed softly. 'Child, the things you come out with.'

'Amelia taught me some things.' I lowered my voice.

'Mama, Amelia taught me my letters and numbers and some words.'

Mama stared at me, her face bathed in the silver moonlight, shining through the trees. 'Did she now...'

'That's until she started listening to Best Friend and decided I wasn't fit to spit on,' I sighed.

'So you can read and write?'

'Some.'

'How come you never told me before?'

'I thought you might get mad at me,' I admitted.

'Well, I'm glad you had sense enough to hide it. The Devil's Best Friend would've chopped off your hands for sure if he thought you could write letters and worse.'

And weren't that the truth. Best Friend would've probably done something to my eyes as well to make sure I couldn't read no more either. That was the kind of less-than-human he was.

Mama got to her feet, pulling me up after her. 'Come on, child. We still have a long, long way to go.'

My heart had only just stopped jumping about in my chest and now here we were, running again.

'Mama, are we running 'cause of me?'

Mama slowed at that. Turning to me she said, 'I wanted to run after you was born. I didn't want another child of mine to be a slave, but your daddy said we should stay together. If we ran and got caught... So I stayed and one winter turned into two and two turned into three. And your daddy was sold away and I told myself that I could bear that if I had you. But I'm not letting Best Friend sell you. I'm not letting you grow up like me. You're much too precious to me to let that happen to you.'

I smiled. 'I love you too, Mama.'

Mama hugged me harder than hard, just for an instant. But then it was over.

'Now that's enough talk,' Mama frowned. 'We have to save our breath for running.'

And we were off again. We ran. But my steps seemed lighter and my heart was not quite so heavy. Not quite. We were going North.

One day later, it wasn't an adventure any more. The adventure side of things had left a long time ago. A lifetime ago. Every owl's hoot, every cracking twig, every shuffle and rustle and murmur put my heart clean up in my mouth. The thrilling, exciting part about running away had faded to nothing. I was scared to death. Scared so I couldn't even summon up enough spit in my bone-dry mouth to swallow. Best Friend was sure to have summoned up all the help he could find to track us down. And we didn't seem to be making much progress. We stuck to the trees for as long as we could and only travelled at night, hiding during the day but the night didn't last long. Night was unbearably short. All the field slaves used to say that when they came back to the slave shack, dragging their feet and hanging their heads with exhaustion, almost too tired to eat what little there was. They'd just fall on to their sacking, wishing the night was twice as long as it was – the way we all did. I knew Mama and I were lucky. We were house slaves. We had it bad enough, but the field slaves had it much worse. But now that Mama and me were on the run, the night time seemed to pass in the blink of an eye.

Mama and I were hiding high up in a tree. In the distance I was sure I could hear dogs barking. I used my hand to wipe the sweat off my forehead. Horrified, I imagined Best Friend and his men standing under the tree, realising why it was raining from the tree and nowhere else. I looked up at Mama.

She smiled at me and whispered, 'Don't worry, child. Even if I don't make it, you surely will.'

'I want to go North with you, Mama,' I protested.

'And you will, honey. But maybe you'll get there before me. If that happens then I'll be along later – I promise.'

'What do we do now?'

'We wait for the night to come,' Mama said softly. 'I reckon in a few more days we'll reach the Ohio river.'

'I'm hungry.' I pressed my hands over my stomach which was rumbling.

Mama dug into her brown sack and took out a red apple. Handing it down to me, she warned. 'Give me the core when you've finished. We don't need to leave behind no clues to help them find us.'

I began to eat the apple the way I always did, with big fat bites.

'Slow, little nibbles,' Mama urged. 'There's not much food left. Make it last.'

'D'you want some, Mama?'

Mama shook her head. It occurred to me that I hadn't seen Mama eat very much of anything since we'd started running.

'Aren't you hungry?'

'Yes, but not for food,' Mama whispered. 'I'm hungry to see my daughter free. I'm hungry to keep one of my children by my side. That no-kind-of-man Best Friend

has already sold three of my children away from me —
like I was a rock or a stone and wouldn't care.'

'I have brothers and sisters?' I stared at her. 'I never
knew that.'

'What was the use in telling you? We neither of us
are ever going to see them again. They've gone and
that's that. But I won't let them take you away from me.
I won't.'

'How many brothers do I have? How many sisters?
What are their names? Where are they...?'

'Child, I don't want to hear another word about
them, d'you hear? I don't know where they are. I try not
to think about them. It tears up my heart to think about
them. So not another word.'

Mama closed her eyes and turned her head. There
were so many things I wanted to ask her but I didn't
speak. I didn't even open my mouth. I suddenly had
brothers and sisters, and not knowing any of them hurt.
It hurt something fierce. I tried and tried but I just
didn't understand what made Best Friend and others
like him hate us so much. And they must surely hate us
to trample us into the dirt the way they did. Who made
the rule that we were less than them because of the
colour of our skin? Was it written down somewhere? In

what book? And who wrote it? I tried and tried but I just couldn't figure it out.

Mama and I both sat in silence for a long time. Mama's eyes were clouded over, like she was in pain but doing her best not to scream out. I wanted to do something to cheer her, but how, when I didn't feel cheered myself?

'What else is in the sack, Mama?'

'A few berries, some bread and a knife in case we're lucky enough to catch a rabbit or some fish.'

I nodded but didn't reply. The knife was to protect us. I'm not stupid. I knew that much. After all, when would we have time for skinning and cleaning and such like? All we had time to do was run, run, run. And hide and be scared and pray. But mostly just run.

I made a mistake. Mama said I wasn't to leave her side no matter what. But I did. I was thirsty. That's what it was. I was thirsty until I thought I'd surely die if I didn't get a mouthful of water – and soon. And what made it worse was that in the distance I could see a well. It was just beyond the edge of some trees, not too far away from a main house. The house wasn't as grand as Best Friend's, I could see that much, but it was the well that had most of my attention. Mama was dozing – one of the few moments since we'd started running that I'd seen her take any kind of rest. I climbed down out of the tree, quiet as an ant with a secret, and headed for the well.

I only had eyes for the well – and that was my mistake. I was close enough to almost smell the water in it, when all at once there came a yapping and howling and barking that sent my heart shooting up towards my ears and plunging back down to my toes. Three snarling, vicious dogs were tied to a fence ring – and in my haste to get some water, I hadn't even seen them. They howled at me, slathering and slobbering and I stared at them, my feet rooted to the ground. The front door of the main house opened. Two white men came out to see what all the dogs' fuss was about.

'You, child!'

I stared at them, realising now just what I'd done.

'Yes, you child. What're you doing there? Who are you?'

One of the men came down the house steps and started walking towards me.

Someone pulled at my arm, pulling me away from the man. Frantically, I turned ready to lash out. It was Mama.

'Run, child. Run!'

Mama and I took off like the wind, darting in and out of the trees around us. I heard calling and shouting and the dogs bark, bark, barking like they were more than ready to tear us apart. Behind us, I heard a sudden yelp, then another and another and knew that the dogs had been released and they were after us. And still Mama and I ran and ran.

The whole world was nothing but a long, hard road to run on. We ran for our lives. I wanted to stop and catch my breath. I wanted to pause and tell Mama I was sorry, but with the dogs chasing us I knew I couldn't. Mama didn't even look at me. She held my hand and pulled me after her as we tried to escape. The dogs behind us were getting closer. Abruptly, Mama stopped. There was no more solid ground. We were at the top of a waterfall with what seemed like a redwood-tree-long drop to the rushing river below.

And behind us, the dogs were getting closer.

'Mama…'

'Jump.'

I opened my mouth, but I'll never know what I was going to say because the next thing I knew we were falling, falling. I managed to let out a scream and then the icy water hit my whole body and filled my mouth.

Down, down, down I went. But that wasn't what frightened me half to death. It was not feeling Mama's hand holding mine. For the first time, I felt alone. I opened my mouth to scream and swallowed half the river. And then I was being dragged up and dragged out. I vomited up everything in my stomach. It felt like I was bringing up the first meal I'd ever had after being a baby. I coughed and spluttered and retched until my whole body shook like someone with the palsy.

'Come on, angel. We must keep going,' Mama panted, her sack still hitched high on one shoulder.

'No, Mama. I can't.' I managed to gasp out. 'I can't. I can't.'

'You must.'

But I wasn't moving. I had no strength to even get to my feet, never mind run. I shook my head, too bone-tired to even argue.

'Look, there's a hollow over there.' Mama pointed across the river. 'It might be a cave. We'll stay there until you've got your strength back.'

Half-staggering and with Mama half-dragging me, we moved down river until it looked shallow enough to wade across. I couldn't hear dogs or men shouting or anything else. Just the river, rushing and roaring like it was mad at us for disturbing it. We finally made it across by jumping and wading. Then we climbed up a steep slope to the hollow Mama thought she'd seen. It was little more than a cut in the rock. It was set back some so that with luck, bad eyesight and darkness we might not be spotted, but I knew we couldn't rely on that. The wind was picking up now, like there was a storm coming. Mama sniffed at the air, then shook her head.

'I'll be all right in a minute, Mama,' I whispered. But it was a lie. I felt sick and was too tired to hide it.

Mama smiled and stroked my face, her callused fingers tender against my skin.

'We'll do fine, sugar,' she whispered back.

But then I heard the dogs. The barking was coming from in front of us. Behind us was the waterfall so we couldn't go back. And across the river was a steep, steep bank. The dogs would be on us before we were more than halfway up. And now I could hear the sound of dogs coming from behind us as well. And where there were dogs there were their owners, white men – the brethren of Best Friend.

'We're not going to make it, are we Mama?'

'It don't seem so.'

And those words were as heavy as the world, bending

my head and bowing my back and breaking my heart.

'Mama, don't let them take me back. I don't never want to go back.'

'You ain't going back, my love. You're going North,' Mama smiled.

'But we're surrounded. They'll take us back and whip us and then Best Friend will sell me...'

The fear I felt was like heavy rocks piled up on top of me. And there was no way out, no way away. I'd seen what Best Friend and his foreman had done to other slaves who dared to run away. They were whipped until what little flesh there was left on their backs hung like strips of meat in the smoke house. I couldn't stand that. I knew I couldn't.

'Mama...'

'Hush, child. Hush. You're going to be free. Didn't I promise you?'

'But...'

'Lean against me and close your eyes.'

I looked at Mama. She had tears in her eyes but the smile she gave me lit my heart. I hugged her tight then turned to lie with my back against her chest.

'Close your eyes and see Heaven, my love,' Mama whispered.

I heard her fish in her sack. And then I knew what

she was looking for. I smiled. And as my smile grew fatter, so my fear grew thinner until it was all but gone. I opened my eyes and saw Mama's knife in her hand. I closed my eyes again.

'I love you, angel,' Mama whispered in my ear.

'I'm going to be free.' I reached out my hands in front of me. I could see freedom, even though my eyes were closed. I could almost touch it. It was only seconds away. I felt nothing but pure, pure joy. Joy like nothing I'd ever felt before. Joy enough to fill the whole wide world. 'I'm going North, Mama. I'm going *North.*'

And Mama's knife moved against my throat.

20th
CENTURY

———★———

MARGARET MAHY

SWIMMING IN TIME

Illustrated by Tim Stevens

MARGARET MAHY

SWIMMING IN TIME

'Come in,' said the angel in the clown-suit and the false nose. 'My nickname is Babel – Bibble-Babble-Babel – because I talk every language ever invented, even the language of the grass, which is a very strange language indeed. But you can call me Babel for short. And since all things in the 20th Century have names, you must have names too. So *you* can be Silver and *you* can be Blue, and *you* can be Green.' He pointed at the last two spirits. 'Purple! Gold! Very rich! Magnificent, really.'

The new spirits felt their names close around them like silken nets and pull them into the shapes of children, all coloured like rainbows. They laughed, stretched out their new arms and wiggled their new fingers. Secretly, they all thought they looked much better than Babel, who seemed kind but somehow empty, as if an important part of him had been left out.

'Are you really an angel?' asked Blue, sounding puzzled.

'Well, I'm not one of the *great* angels,' said Babel, turning a somersault. 'Definitely not an archangel. But I'm not a Fallen Angel either. There's a certain miserable grandeur about being one of the Fallen. But I'm a clown-angel – always a clown-angel – because of something I once decided.'

'What did you decide?' asked Gold, making up his mind to decide differently.

'Forget me!' said Babel. 'Think about yourselves! You want to be born, and you've all chosen the 20th Century. Right?'

Silver laughed with pleasure. 'I like the look of it. I like that big 2 that starts off like a question mark, but flattens out along the bottom. A question mark wobbles on one leg and a little dot, but 2 stands firmly.'

'Like a teapot on a teapot stand,' said Babel, beaming.

'No! No! Don't ask me what a teapot is. You'll find out soon enough. The 20th Century is full of teapots.'

'*I* like the zero,' said Purple. 'It looks like an egg, and wonderful things hatch out of eggs.'

The other three spirits danced and wiggled their new fingers.

'Good! Good!' said Babel. 'Now my job is to tumble you towards the 20th Century. I should warn you – it *is* dangerous.'

'That makes it exciting,' said Silver.

'Oh yes – exciting!' agreed Babel. 'And dangerous!'

He clapped his hands. The space in front of him opened like a smiling mouth, pushing out what might have been lips.

'Follow me!' shouted Babel and somersaulted through that mouth. The rainbow children followed him. Suddenly they were swimming in time – even swallowing it. Tick-tock, tick-tock, it went inside them.

Below them lay the world, swimming in time too.

'Now,' said Babel. 'Here we are, at the beginning of the 20th Century.'

The 20th Century looked like a glittering silver ribbon tied round the world, holding it together. 'Oh, look! 1901!' cried Babel. 'An airship. The first Zeppelin! People flying.

A good beginning!'

Something pushed out through the glitter of time. The first Zeppelin rose like a balloon into the sky. The children could see the people standing below it, small but lively, watching it rise, all of them thrilled with what they were seeing.

Almost immediately Purple was distracted, for part of the silver ribbon below seemed to split open and she could see right through it.

'What's going on over there?' she cried, pointing. 'Look at all that rushing about... that rising up into the air...'

'They're racing! They're jumping!' Babel jumped too. He rose into space, then flipped over and over on his way down again. 'It's what they call the Olympic Games. They were in Paris that year. Look carefully. It's the first time women have been allowed to take part in the Olympic Games. Oh, the 20th Century is going to be a good century for women.'

'Not for those women!' cried Green pointing in yet another direction. '*They* don't look as if they are enjoying the 20th Century much. And what's that red stuff oozing out of those men?'

'Blood!' said Babel. 'Probably blood. Oh yes, I see now. It *is* blood. Those men are killing each other. And the women and children are prisoners who are starving. It's a war – the Boer War. Terrible!'

'Why are they fighting?' asked Green.

'Oh, they're just arguing about who really owns the land and who should set the rules for running it,' said Babel carelessly. 'People have argued about that for hundreds of years.'

'Who *does* own the land?' asked Blue.

'Nobody owns it,' said Babel. 'People chop and change the boundaries, but the land owns itself.'

'But whose fault is it?' asked Purple uneasily. 'The war, I mean.'

'Oh well, as to *fault*,' said Babel, 'you don't have to worry about faults yet. Don't be anxious until you have to be. Now, look at that line of light over there! Two thousand miles of it... That's the first radio message speeding from Cornwall in England to Newfoundland on the other side of the Atlantic. What a wonderful century you've chosen to be born in.'

'There goes a little animal in a blue coat,' cried Gold.

'Peter Rabbit!' exclaimed Babel. 'Beatrix Potter wrote about him in 1902. He's going to run all the way through the 20th Century. And here comes 1903! That's the first aeroplane you can see flying there. The Wright brothers were the first to fly, you know!'

'And in 1904 people learned to fly by themselves,' cried Silver, looking ahead.

'Fly by themselves?' said Babel, puzzled. 'Never!' But then he saw a little figure swooping and soaring above the glitter. 'Of course!' he cried. 'It's Peter Pan, the hero of a famous play that turned into an even more famous book. Peter first flew in 1904, and he's been flying ever since.'

The children danced around Babel, and he danced too, pointing out interesting things in the 20th Century. 'There was the great scientist, Albert Einstein. There was the terrible earthquake in San Francisco. People wrote wonderful books and painted wonderful pictures. In 1908 a scientist called Ernest Rutherford won a Nobel Prize for describing how atoms were put together. And in 1911 the explorer, Amundsen, finally reached the South Pole! He *walked* all the way.'

The spirits cheered and Babel turned a somersault.

'But what's that darkness?' cried Gold, suddenly sounding terrified, for an oily blackness was pushing its way through the glitter below them.

'That!' said Babel. 'Oh that!' His voice grew troubled for a moment. 'You're looking too far ahead. That is 1914 – the First World War. Ten million dead! Pity!'

'Another war!' said Gold, feeling stunned. 'Is it about land again?'

'The same dreary old quarrels,' said Babel. He twisted his false nose. 'But hey! Remember the good things! See? Scientists are discovering insulin! Wonderful! It will help people with a dreadful illness called diabetes. And over there, John Logie Baird is finding a way of transmitting pictures by wireless. You know what that's going to lead to, don't you? Television!' He beamed, pulled his nose away from his face and let it bounce back again as he added, 'It's January 1926 already. Of course it takes a while to get going, but when it does...'

'Who *is* that man with the little black moustache?' interrupted Gold. 'The one doing all that shouting?'

'Him? Oh, his name is Hitler,' said Babel. 'He'll be important in a year or two. But for now concentrate on that wonderful dancer leaping and bending... beautiful as a swan. Her name is Anna Pavlova. She is a ballerina. And don't miss that bear wandering in between the pine trees humming and dreaming. His name is Winnie the Pooh – just as remarkable in his own way as Anna Pavlova. Whoops! We're into 1927.'

'There are the Wright brothers again,' said Purple as

a tiny aeroplane rose above the glitter and darkness of the 20th Century.

'No, no!' said Babel. 'That's Charles Lindbergh, the first man to fly solo across the Atlantic Ocean. Isn't it amazing? The aeroplane has only been invented for such a few years and people are already flying such great distances.'

But the spirits had suddenly seen something ahead of them. They had stopped dancing and wiggling their fingers.

'It's war again,' cried Purple. 'It is! It is! Look at it, spreading like horrible, stinking oil.'

'Yes,' Babel sighed. 'That *is* war – the Second World War. A lot of countries were part of it – Germany, France, the British Isles, the USA, Japan, Australia, New Zealand, Russia...'

The black ooze suddenly split as if something was pushing its way through from beneath. A terrible glare lit the whole century. The spirits cowered back without asking a single question.

Babel sighed. 'And that's the atomic bomb!' he said.

The spirits were quiet.

'What a terrible century!' said Blue at last.

'They all seem so sure of themselves,' said Green, and

his voice had a trace of envy in it.

'Remember the good things!' exclaimed Babel. 'Glance back into 1928! See? There's Alexander Fleming at St Mary's Hospital in London. He's discovering penicillin, which will save millions of lives.'

'But he's discovering it by accident,' said Gold. 'Does that still count?'

'Chance and chaos are part of the universe,' said Babel, spinning on one toe like a question mark.

'Babel,' said Blue, 'I know there are good things going on. But what about all these wars? What about that atomic bomb? Look at all those people burnt and dying – even the little children. And if you look ahead people are still dying years later because that bomb made them so ill.'

'But after the Second World War people make up their minds that they can do better – they *will* do better,' said Babel comfortingly. 'There they are in that tall building with hundreds of windows. It's called the United Nations.'

'Were they united after that?' asked Silver.

'Well, not exactly,' Babel replied cautiously. 'But it certainly did some good.'

'No, it didn't! Wars go on and on and on,' declared

Green. 'I can see them. There's one, in 1950.'

'Korea! Yes,' said Babel. 'Korea split in two. But Disneyland opened in 1955, and millions of people have enjoyed themselves in Disneyland. And there's Rosa Parks... a real heroine for you! She was a black woman in the States who refused to leave that part of the bus marked for white people only. It was so brave of her... so very brave. The world began to change for the better because of people like Rosa Parks. And then in 1956, things really began to rock and roll! That man with the guitar – that's Elvis Presley. Look at everyone dancing!'

'Dancing!' cried Gold indignantly. 'We're worried about the wars, and all you talk about is dancing.'

'Babel, what are those black smudges there, and there, and there?' cried Purple.

Babel pulled his clown hat down as far as his false nose.

'More wars!' he mumbled under the hat. 'Cambodia! And Vietnam! And Serbia... Biafra... Israel... Jordan... Angola. The difficulty is that being alive is just not *safe*. If it isn't war, it's disasters such as tidal waves and earthquakes. A tidal wave killed 150,000 people in Pakistan. You can see it happening in 1970. And in 1972 an earthquake in Nicaragua killed ten thousand people.'

'War's worse,' said Blue.

'Much worse!' agreed Babel. 'But don't forget the triumphs. Look at 1969. There! Didn't I tell you? Space travel! Man setting foot on the moon! A giant step for mankind. And all the time jokes kept coming into the world from nowhere. Would you like me to tell you a few jokes?'

'No!' said Gold. 'I don't want to have anything to do with any joke that comes out of the 20th Century. I don't want to be born. I don't want to have a name.'

And his child shape, with its smiles and frowns and lively fingers melted into a shapeless mist. Giving up their names, the other spirits shivered and melted too.

Down below them the silver ribbon of the 20th Century began to writhe as if it were in pain. Darkness and still more darkness seeped out of it.

'What's happening to the 20th Century?' cried one of the spirits.

'Take no notice,' Babel cried back. 'You're entitled to say you don't want to be born. That's what I said too.'

'But why has the 20th Century got worse?' asked a spirit.

Babel coughed in a slightly embarrassed way.

'It's because one of you has decided not to be born,'

he said. 'Or all of you! Losing certain people makes a big difference to a century. A lot of little differences can add up to a big change.'

'Do you mean we are important?' cried a nameless spirit. 'Us?'

'Of course!' said Babel. 'Remember, a butterfly flapping its wings can sometimes cause a hurricane at sea.'

The spirits flowed into one another. They all became a single colour... a colour for which there was no name because it was never seen by people who needed to name things. Below them the 20th Century writhed in agony.

At last the spirits split into their separate selves once more. They pulled the silken nets of their names around themselves again, turned back into rainbow children, and floated back towards Babel.

'It's hard, being born,' said Silver, 'but if it makes a difference we will agree to be born. We've decided.'

Babel gave a shout, turning a somersault.

'Right on!' he cried. 'And who knows? If you're strong... if you're true... those black patches may shrink and fade. I know it's not easy.' He hesitated. 'I told you. I had the chance once – to be born I mean. But I – well – I backed off.'

'Did things change because you decided not to be born?' asked Gold.

'Did they change for good?' asked Blue. 'Or bad?'

Suddenly Babel hid his face in his hands.

'You did say you weren't a Fallen Angel,' said Green nervously.

'Oh, I'm good,' said Babel through his fingers. 'Only not as good as I could have been. And two centuries later the little difference I would have made grew to be a big one.' He looked up. 'Are you all sure?'

'I am!' said Silver.

'We all are!' said Gold.

Babel and the beautiful children looked down at the earth again. The 20th Century held it closely. It still had its dark patches, but, in amid the darkness, it shone. They swam in time, drinking in that shining.

'Well, then,' sighed Babel at last. 'On you go! You know the way. And good luck!'

The beautiful children – the blue, the green, the purple, the gold and silver – drifted away from him, touching his hand with gentle fingers as they slid by.

Left on his own, Babel took off his false nose. He lingered a moment, still looking down at the world.

'Shall I spy a little?' he asked himself. 'Shall I?'

Below him the silver ribbon of the 20th Century suddenly opened an eye. It became a wonderful dragon with an eye as deep as midnight — an eye that held a thousand other universes. The eye winked at Babel.

He put out his hand, felt around in the space in front of him, then made a movement as if he were turning the page of an invisible book. Light came out of nowhere. It burst into his face like sudden sunshine so that Babel looked, just for a moment, even in his clown-suit, as beautiful as a true archangel.

'The 21st Century!' he cried. 'What a beauty. What a wonderful new century they're making down there.'

Then he let the invisible page fall, stepped back through the mouth of time, and disappeared.

ABOUT THE AUTHORS

✦

BERNARD ASHLEY was a headteacher for many years before becoming a full-time writer. His first novel *The Trouble with Donovan Croft* won the Children's Rights Workshop Other Award. His novel *Dodgem*, which he serialised for television, won the Royal Television Society Award for best children's programme and he and his son, Chris, wrote a serial for Granada television *Three, Seven, Eleven*. His novels for older children include *Tiger Without Teeth, Johnny's Blitz* and *Little Soldier* and for younger children, *Dinner Ladies Don't Count* and *King Rat*. Bernard Ashley was born in Woolwich, South London and now lives less than a mile away in Charlton.

✦

MALORIE BLACKMAN was a database manager and systems programmer before becoming a full-time writer. Her novel *Hacker* won the W H Smith's Mind Boggling Books Award and the Young Telegraph Children's Book of the Year Award. *Thief* also won the Young Telegraph Children's Book of the Year Award and *Pigheart Boy* won an UKRA award. Her other novels include *Dangerous Reality, Whizziwig*, made into a successful BBC Television series, *Jack Sweettooth the 73rd* and *Tell Me No Lies*. Malorie Blackman lives in South East London with her husband and their young daughter.

✦

HENRIETTA BRANFORD had many jobs before becoming a full-time writer and the characters in her novels are all based on people she met or had heard about. *Dimanche Diller* won the Smarties Prize and *Fire, Bed and Bone* won The Guardian Award. Her other novels include *The Fated Sky, Dimanche Diller in Danger, Dimanche Diller at Sea, Spacebaby, Spacebaby and the Megavolt Monster* and for younger readers *Ruby Red* and the picture book *Little Pig Figwort*. Henrietta Branford was born in India. She lived with her husband, the photographer Paul Carter, and their three children in Southampton. She died at home, from breast cancer, on April 23rd, 1999.

✦

THERESA BRESLIN is a professional librarian as well as an author. Her first book, *Simon's Challenge*, won the Kathleen Fidler Award for children's literature and was filmed for television. Other novels include *New School Blues, Across the Roman Wall* and *Different Directions* which was dramatised for radio. *Death or Glory Boys* won the longer novel category of the Sheffield Book Award, *Kezzie* was shortlisted for the Children's Book Award and *Whispers in the Graveyard* won the Carnegie Medal. Her more recent titles are *The Dream*

Master and *Starship Rescue*. Theresa Breslin was born in central Scotland and still lives there.

★

MELVIN BURGESS was a trainee journalist, a casual labourer and a dyer of silk before becoming a full-time writer. His first book *The Cry of the Wolf* was published in 1990. His other titles include *An Angel for May, The Baby and Fly Pie, The Earth Giant, Kite, Tiger Tiger, Burning Izzy, The Copper Treasure* and *Bloodtide*. He won the Carnegie Medal and The Guardian Fiction Award for *Junk*. Melvin Burgess was born in London, brought up in Sussex and Berkshire and now lives in Manchester.

★

GILLIAN CROSS has been a baker's assistant, a childminder and a constituency assistant to an MP. Her first books for children were *The Runaway* and *The Iron Way,* published in 1979. She won the Carnegie Medal for *Wolf,* the Whitbread Children's Novel Award and the Smarties Prize for *The Great Elephant Chase.* She is the author of many books including *Tightrope, Dark Behind the Curtain,* and *The Demon Headmaster* and *The Prime Minister's Brain*, successfully serialised by the BBC. Gillian Cross is a great supporter of libraries and has served on national committees and working parties in support of these institutions. Gillian was born in Wembley, London and now lives in Warwickshire.

★

ANNIE DALTON has worked as a waitress, a cleaner, a factory worker and is now a full-time writer. Her book *The Afterdark Princess* won the Nottinghamshire Book Award and its sequel *The Dream Snatcher* has been published recently. *Night Maze* was shortlisted for the Carnegie Medal as was *The Real Tilly Beany*. *Naming the Dark* and *Swan Sister* were shortlisted for the Sheffield Children's Book Award. Other books include *Out of the Ordinary* and *The Alpha Box*. Annie Dalton was born in Dorset and now lives in Suffolk.

★

ALAN DURANT is a copywriter for a children's publisher as well as being an author. His books for teenagers include *Blood, Publish or Die* and *A Short Stay in Purgatory*. His stories for younger children include *Little Troll, Spider McDrew, Creepe Hall*, the Leggs United series and picture books *Big Fish, Little Fish, Snake Supper* and *Hector Sylvester.* Alan Durant was born in Sutton, Surrey and lived in Oxford, Paris and London before settling in New Malden with his wife and three children.

★

VIVIAN FRENCH worked in children's theatre for ten years before she established herself as a storyteller. In 1988 she began to write for children and has written numerous books since then. Highlights include *Caterpillar*

Caterpillar, which was shortlisted for the Emil/Kurt Maschler Award, and *A Song for Little Toad* which was shortlisted for the Smarties Prize. For older children she has written *Aesop's Funky Fables*, *Kickback* and, under the name of Louis Catt, two stories in the *Sleepover Club* series. She has travelled from Orkney to Oklahoma talking about children's books; is a visiting lecturer at the University of the West of England and reviews for the *Guardian*.

✦

ADÈLE GERAS taught French at a girls' grammar school and started writing in 1973. Her first book, *Tea at Mrs Manderby's*, was published in 1976. Her books include *silent snow, secret snow*, *A Candle in the Dark*, *The Gingerbread House*, *Voyage* and the forthcoming *Troy*. Her books for younger readers include *Chalk and Cheese* and the series *The Cats of Cuckoo Square*. Her prize-winning short story collections have now been published as *Stories from Jerusalem*. Adèle Geras was born in Jerusalem and travelled widely as a child. Married with two children, she lives in Manchester.

✦

MARY HOFFMAN has written more than seventy books for children. She is the author of the award-winning *Amazing Grace* and *Grace and Family*. Her other books include *Song of the Earth*, *Sun, Moon and Stars*, *An Angel Just Like Me* and *Three Wise Women*. Mary Hoffman is a tireless campaigner for libraries, locally and nationally. She also produces a children's books newsletter called *Armadillo*. She was born in Hampshire and now lives in North London with her husband and three daughters.

✦

PETE JOHNSON has been a film critic for Radio One, a journalist and a teacher. He has written several novels for teenagers including *Ten Hours to Live*, *We The Haunted* and *The Protectors*. His spooky stories have earned special acclaim. They include *Eyes of the Alien*, *The Phantom Thief*, *My Friend's a Werewolf* and *The Ghost Dog* which won the Young Telegraph Award and the Stockton Children's Book of the Year Award. Other popular titles include *Mind Reader* and *Secret Friend*. Pete Johnson was born in Hampshire and now lives in Hertfordshire.

✦

MARGARET MAHY has been a nurse, a librarian and is New Zealand's best-known children's author. She became the first writer outside the United Kingdom to win the Carnegie Medal for *The Haunting*, winning the same award two years later for *The Changeover*. Her other novels include *Operation Terror*, *The Five Sisters*, *The Other Side of Silence* and *A Villain's Night Out*. Her books for younger children include *The Great Piratical Rumbustification* and *The Great White Man-eating Shark*. In 1993 she was awarded New Zealand's highest honour, the Order of New

Zealand, which is only ever held by twenty living people at any one time.

✶

GERALDINE McCAUGHREAN writes fiction for adults, early readers and every age in between. Her novel *A Little Lower Than the Angels* won the Whitbread Children's Novel Award; *A Pack of Lies* won the Carnegie Medal and the Guardian Children's Fiction Award. Fifty other books include *Plundering Paradise, Forever X, The Stones are Hatching*, re-tellings of *Moby Dick, Roman Myths, Pilgrims Progress* and four volumes of myths and legends from around the world. Geraldine McCaughrean was born in London and now lives in Berkshire with husband John and daughter Ailsa.

✶

MICHAEL MORPURGO is the author of over sixty books for children including *The Butterfly Lion*, winner of the Smarties Prize and the Writers' Guild Award, and *The Wreck of the Zanzibar* which won the Whitbread Award and was the IBBY Honour Book of 1998. His other titles include *The Dancing Bear, Farm Boy*, the *Mudpuddle Farm* books in the Jets series, and picture books *Sam's Duck* and *Wombat Goes Walkabout*. Michael lives in Devon with his wife Clare. Together they established Farms for City Children and were awarded the MBE in recognition of their services to youth through this organisation.

✶

JENNY NIMMO has been an actor, researcher, floor-manager and script editor for children's television. Her first book *The Bronze Trumpeter* was published in 1975. *The Snow Spider* – the first title in a fantasy trilogy – won the Tir na n'Og award and the Smarties Grand Prix. Her other novels include *The Witch's Tears, The Owl Tree*, winner of the Smarties gold medal for younger children, *Griffin's Castle*, and for older readers *The Rinaldi Ring*. Jenny Nimmo was born in Berkshire and now lives and works in Wales with her artist husband and three bi-lingual children.

✶

JEREMY STRONG has been a headteacher, teacher, caretaker, strawberry picker and a jam doughnut stuffer! His first book was *Smith's Tail*, published in 1978. Since then he has written many books including *The Karate Princess, Dinosaur Pox, Fatbag; The Demon Vacuum Cleaner, There's a Pharoah in my Bed*, and *Viking at School*. He won the Children's Book Award for *The Hundred-Mile-an-Hour Dog*. His work is characterised by its humour and direct child appeal. Jeremy Strong was born in Eltham, South East London. He now lives in Kent.

✶

ROBERT SWINDELLS was in the RAF for three years, then had a variety of jobs including shop assistant, clerk, printer and engineer. He trained as a teacher and subsequently taught for eight years before becoming a full-time writer. He won the Children's Rights Workshop Other Award with *Brother in the Land* which also won the Children's Book Award. He won the Children's Book Award again with *Room 13* and, in the shorter novel category, for *Nightmare Stairs*. He won the Carnegie Medal for *Stone Cold* and the Angus Book Award for *Unbeliever*. Robert Swindells was born in Bradford and now lives on the Yorkshire Moors with his wife, Brenda.

✶

JEAN URE began writing at the age of six, but had to wait until she was sixteen to have her first book published! She went to the Webber Douglas Academy of Dramatic Art and her love of ballet and theatre have inspired many of her books, not least the acclaimed *A Proper Little Nooryeff*. Her novels for older readers include *Skinny Melon and Me*, *Becky Bananas* and *Fruit and Nutcase*; *Love is Forever*, *Just Sixteen* and the *Plague* trilogy, the first book of which won the Lancashire Book Award. For younger readers she has written *Whistle and I'll Come,* winner of the Stockton Children's Award, *Help! It's Harriet* and *The Puppy Present,* shortlisted for the Children's Book Award, and the series *We Love Animals.* Jean was born in Surrey where she still lives, in a three-hundred-year-old house, with her husband and their family of rescued dogs and cats. She is a vegan and is committed to animal rights.

✶

JACQUELINE WILSON had her first story published when she was seventeen and was a journalist for several years before taking up full-time writing. She has written more than thirty children's books including *The Story of Tracy Beaker* which won the Nottinghamshire Oak Tree Award and the Sheffield Children's Book Award; *The Suitcase Kid*, winner of the Children's Book Award; *The Bed and Breakfast Star*, winner of the Young Telegraph Award and *Double Act*, winner of the Smarties Prize and the Children's Book Award. Jacqueline Wilson has one grown-up daughter and lives in Surrey in a small house crammed with 10,000 books!

━━━✶━━━